CW01239288

Cameras, Combat and Courage

In Memoriam – Bill Mondjack

Sadly, Bill Mondjack passed away a short time before this book came into being. Luckily for me and several others that tell their stories here, we had the opportunity to know and work with Bill in Vietnam. He will be missed by friends, family, and all of us that served with him.

Bill arrived in Vietnam right around the same time that I and several others did, to join the 69th Signal Battalion at Tan Son Nhut Airbase just outside Saigon.

Bill, like me, was an "84G" – the military designation for a Photo Lab Technician. We shared many hours in the 69th's photo lab at Camp Gaylor, churning out thousands of black-and-white prints and processing Ektachrome transparency film rolls.

Bill at Camp Gaylor, ready to head back to the States in September 1967. And yes, he's added a 35mm Nikon to his arsenal of cameras!

Bill seemed a bit on the shy and quiet side at first, but eventually his sense of humor broke through and he even became the occasional prankster, like many of us, on and off duty.

We also shared occasional trips to downtown Saigon, Bill lugging his beloved personal camera, a cumbersome Mamiya C-Series twin-lens reflex that took large-format 2 and 1/4-inch frames. I don't think I ever saw him with any other camera than the Mamiya …

Bill was a great photographer and, after the Army, he returned to Pennsylvania where he and his wife Carol ran a successful photography business. He also became an avid beekeeper and honey producer and that was a second successful business.

I am proud that Bill shared his story in these pages. His chapter is "My Story: Vietnam 1966–1967."

RIP, brother … we will all miss you.

Combat Photographer Willy Muchler (left) and I visited Bill (right) at his Pennsylvania home in July 2013. It was the last time I ever saw him. Willy's story, "An Angel On My Shoulder," is also in this book.

Cameras, Combat and Courage

The Vietnam War By The Military's Own Photographers

Dan Brookes

Pen & Sword
MILITARY

First published in Great Britain in 2019 by
Pen & Sword Military
An imprint of
Pen & Sword Books Ltd
Yorkshire – Philadelphia

Copyright © Dan Brookes, 2019

ISBN 978 1 52675 023 5

The right of Dan Brookes to be identified as Author of this work has been asserted by him in accordance with the Copyright, Designs and Patents Act 1988.

A CIP catalogue record for this book is
available from the British Library.

All rights reserved. No part of this book may be reproduced or transmitted in any form or by any means, electronic or mechanical including photocopying, recording or by any information storage and retrieval system, without permission from the Publisher in writing.

Printed and bound in India by Replika Press Pvt. Ltd.

Pen & Sword Books Limited incorporates the imprints of Atlas, Archaeology, Aviation, Discovery, Family History, Fiction, History, Maritime, Military, Military Classics, Politics, Select, Transport, True Crime, Air World, Frontline Publishing, Leo Cooper, Remember When, Seaforth Publishing, The Praetorian Press, Wharncliffe Local History, Wharncliffe Transport, Wharncliffe True Crime and White Owl.

For a complete list of Pen & Sword titles please contact

PEN & SWORD BOOKS LIMITED
47 Church Street, Barnsley, South Yorkshire, S70 2AS, England
E-mail: enquiries@pen-and-sword.co.uk
Website: www.pen-and-sword.co.uk

Or

PEN AND SWORD BOOKS
1950 Lawrence Rd, Havertown, PA 19083, USA
E-mail: Uspen-and-sword@casematepublishers.com
Website: www.penandswordbooks.com

This book contains graphic images that some readers may find disturbing.

Contents

Acknowledgements	vi
Foreword	vii
Introduction by Dan Brookes	x
Vignettes	1
An Angel On My Shoulder by William "Wild Bill" Muchler	3
Unforgettable Experience – Unforgettable Brothers by Roy "Mac" McClellan	21
THE DEATH OF fear by Curtis D. Hicks (Rose)	39
My Story – Vietnam 1966–1967 by William Mondjack	49
What Doesn't Kill You Makes You Stronger by Tom Wong	65
From Phnom Penh to Ripcord: The Free Range Motion Picture Photographer by Christopher Jensen	87
Vietnam – Combat Photography 101 – f/8 and Pray by James Saller	125
Marvin J. Wolf	143
Our Friendly Neighborhood VC Sniper by Marvin J. Wolf	147
Above and Beyond: The Story of Cpl. William T. Perkins, Jr. USMC by Craig Ingraham	154
Operation *Medina* – The Ultimate Sacrifice	158
Ghostriders 079	174
Parting Shots – Afterword	210

Acknowledgements

This book would not have been possible without a myriad of friends and family, from the brothers who served alongside me in Vietnam, to those who guided it along the route from a rough idea to a published book.

I thank John White, fellow Vietnam veteran, mentor, and literary agent, for his expert input, guidance, and extreme patience with me.

I appreciate all the feedback and encouragement from family and friends: My dear friend and companion Marion Bouffard, and three excellent writers, my daughters Marissa and Melanie, and my dear friend, Gary Carlson. Others who responded so kindly to my constant badgering to review my work as it progressed include my aunt, Lucy Brookes, my sister, Carol Hageman, and my nephew, Coulson Hageman, who also aided me in my quest for the very first images of war photography. A special thank you goes to Alesia LeDuc for her thorough proofreading and corrections.

Special thanks also go to my fellow veterans, members of the 221st Signal Company and 69th Signal Battalion, who through the magic of today's social media, were there with feedback and answers to questions about our shared experiences in Vietnam.

I am also grateful to my senior editor Chris Evans and Pen & Sword Books for believing in this book and bringing it life.

But most of all, I'd like to offer my greatest appreciation to all of the other writers and contributors in this book, who were willing and brave enough to relive the most challenging, difficult, and sometimes horrifying moments of their lives. Thank you for digging so deep and going there with me.

Dan Brookes

Foreword

By Joe Galloway

*"The Brave Ones Fought with Weapons.
The Crazy Ones Fought with Cameras."*

Craig Ingraham

From beginning to end the Vietnam War was captured on film in searing images, some of them so powerful that they helped turn a nation's face away from the war it was fighting halfway around the world. Those images are iconic – Nick Ut's photo of the naked little girl fleeing a napalm strike; Eddie Adams' photo of the South Vietnamese general shooting a captured Viet Cong officer in the head on the streets of Saigon.

We all know about the civilian photographers who covered the war. Their images were printed on the front pages every day. Their film stories aired on the nightly network news every day. Dozens of them died alongside the soldiers and Marines they accompanied in battle.

But there were other photographers and film cameramen who covered the war. Their photographs and film were as little known then as they are even today. They were the combat cameramen of the U.S. Army and U.S. Marines who took the same risks, paid the same price but did it for a PFC's or a Buck Sergeant's pay.

Dan Brookes and the late Bob Hillerby reconnected nearly fifty years after they were together in Vietnam, and decided to tell some of the stories and show some of the images of those uniformed shooters before they were lost to history. The results of that determination and several years of hard work gathering the stories and collecting the pictures in two volumes, are this volume, compiled by Dan, *Cameras, Combat and Courage*, as well as the companion volume that preceded it, *Shooting Vietnam*, authored by Dan and Bob together.

On the worst day of my life, in the bloodiest battle of the war, on November 15, 1965, in Landing Zone XRay in the Ia Drang Valley, we were surrounded by North Vietnamese regulars determined to kill us all. The air was filled with bullets and shrapnel and I was hugging the earth. Out of the corner of my eye I noticed two men with cameras nearby, also hugging the ground. Later, during a lull in the fighting,

I saw them filming the battalion surgeon, Dr. Robert Carrera, as he did an urgent tracheotomy on a badly wounded soldier.

The two of them, Sgt. Jack Yamaguchi and Sgt. Thomas Schiro, were from the Department of the Army Special Photographic Office (DASPO). They were shooting silent color film of the battle with an old Bell and Howell 16mm windup camera. Their film would be shipped back to the Pentagon, edited and released to the networks. They had risked their lives and captured priceless film of a historic battle. You might expect they would win some praise; maybe another stripe. Hardly. Their bosses in the Pentagon reprimanded Yamaguchi and Schiro for portraying so grim and bloody a story.

More than two decades later, my co-author, Lt. Gen. Hal Moore, and I would locate the 17 minutes of film shot by Yamaguchi and Schiro, stashed away in the Military Film Archives at Norton Airbase, California. Much of the services' combat film from Vietnam had been deposited in those archives. Not long after we obtained a professional high-tech copy of the Ia Drang film, the Air Force decided to shut down the Archive to save money. The services were invited to reclaim what film they wanted. The rest went to a landfill. The original Ia Drang film was lost or destroyed.

Much of the U.S. Army photos shot by contributors to *Cameras, Combat and Courage* and *Shooting Vietnam* and many of their colleagues in the Signal Corps or in Division public affairs units ended up in the Army Pictorial Center. When a former photo team lieutenant went to search for Vietnam images he found that Congressional budget cuts had forced the archivists – who were working to catalog images from 1944/World War II – to give up some of their leased warehouse space. They decided that any negative that did not have a complete caption – name of photographer, location, unit in shot – would be destroyed. That amounted to 90 percent of the negatives that were shredded.

What has been saved and printed in both this book and *Shooting Vietnam* are photographic prints that the combat cameramen stashed away or mailed home from Vietnam – or come from images they shot with their own personal cameras on their own film. Thank God!

These images run the gamut from combat operations, the lives lived by soldiers and Marines, scenes of Vietnamese civilian life and street scenes. They and the stories told by these men are worthy of your attention. They shed a different light on that war of our youth and we owe Dan Brookes and Bob Hillerby a debt of gratitude for saving something of their legacy from the landfill bulldozers.

Joseph L. Galloway, War Correspondent
Co-author:
We Were Soldiers Once … and Young, We Are Soldiers Still, and *Triumph Without Victory: A History of the Persian Gulf War*

Editor's Note: General (retired) H. Norman Schwarzkopf stated that Joe Galloway is "The finest combat correspondent of our generation – a soldier's reporter and a soldier's friend."

Recalling the fierce battle of the Ia Drang Valley in Vietnam in November of 1965, Lt. Gen. (retired) Hal Moore stated, "I looked over and saw Joe Galloway sitting with his back against a small tree, camera in his lap, rifle across his knees. I knew why I was there. I'm a professional military man and it's my job. But what the hell was HE doing there? Turned out he was doing his job too."

From the We Were Soldiers website: "On May 1, 1998, the Army awarded Galloway a belated Bronze Star with V for rescuing a badly wounded soldier under heavy fire in the Ia Drang Valley on 15 November 1965. His is the only such medal of valor awarded to a civilian by the Army during the Vietnam War."

The book, *We Were Soldiers Once … and Young*, co-authored by Joe and Lt. General Hal Moore recounted that battle. In 2002 it became a feature film with Mel Gibson as Moore and Barry Pepper as Joe Galloway. Many consider it one of the best and most accurate portrayals of the war in Vietnam.

I am proud to have Joe Galloway as a friend and brother-in-arms.

Dan Brookes

Left: A young Joe Galloway as a War Correspondent for UPI (United Press International) during the Vietnam War.

Right: Today, Joe Galloway continues to write and speak at numerous veterans' and other gatherings throughout the country. He is also Special Consultant to the Vietnam War 50th Anniversary Commemoration project at the Department of Defense, Office of the Secretary of Defense. He and his wife Gracie live in North Carolina.

Photo by Steve Northup.

Photo by Chuck Kennedy/KnightRidder.

Introduction

Dan Brookes

"I think the best war photos I have taken have always been made when a battle was actually taking place; when people were confused and scared and courageous and stupid and showed all these things. When you look at people at the moment of truth, everything is quite human."

Horst Faas

This is the first known battlefield photo ever taken. It depicts U.S. Army Major Lucien Webster's artillery battery after the Battle of Buena Vista, February 22 and 23, 1847, during the Mexican-American War. Who took it is a mystery. The photographer is unknown.

Introduction   xi

I get to hold history in my hands. These are the first known war photographs ever taken and are from the Mexican–American War of 1846–1848. (*Courtesy of the Yale Western Americana Collection, Beinecke Rare Book and Manuscript Library, Yale University, New Haven, Connecticut*)

I was privileged to be able to hold this daguerreotype in my hands.

When you hold an actual daguerreotype, you are holding the same piece of metal that the photographer once held when he inserted it into his camera. It was upon that same piece of metal that the photograph would be captured, developed, and live forever. It was right there, on the battlefield, just like a sword, bullet, or scrap of a uniform, one hundred and sixty-plus years ago.

These first battlefield photographs were taken less than ten years after Daguerre announced his photographic process to the world on January 7, 1839.

One witness to Daguerre's announcement was the American, Samuel F. B. Morse, in France at the time in order to secure a French patent for his invention, the electric telegraph. Morse also had been experimenting with the photographic process. Excited by Daguerre's progress, he wrote in an article by the *New York Observer* that it was "… one of the most beautiful discoveries of the age."

But in the years to come, that "beautiful discovery" would be utilized to record the ugliness and horror of war.

xii Cameras, Combat and Courage

Many of the greatest images of the Vietnam War, the most photographed war ever, came from the lenses of a long list of civilian shooters. Horst Faas, Henri Huet, Larry Burrows, and their numerous colleagues produced some of the finest war photographs ever. And then there are also the most iconic of images, like the Eddie Adams photo of a Viet Cong prisoner being executed by the chief of police on a Saigon street, or perhaps the single most memorable image, that of nine-year-old Kim Phúc, running down a road, burned by napalm, taken by Nick Ut; it earned him a Pulitzer Prize.

But behind the scenes, and unheralded for their camera work, were hundreds of military photographers, just doing what was expected of them as a part of their day-to-day job description. Unlike their famous civilian counterparts, many had to endure a year-long assignment that constantly placed them in harm's way. Sometimes it meant dropping the camera and picking up an M-16 or grenade launcher, or manning an M-60 machinegun, or helping to carry the wounded to a medevac dust-off chopper. Like they told us in Basic training, "Your primary MOS (Military Occupational Specialty – your 'job' in the military) is Eleven Bravo (11B): Infantryman!" In other words, regardless of whether you eventually became a cook, mechanic – or photographer, your first duty, and what you were all trained for in Basic, when necessary, was to fire a weapon and kill the enemy.

From 1962 to 1975, military photographers took millions of photographs in Vietnam. Their official mission was to document the war and capture images for the historical record. But more often, their cameras recorded the lives of their fellow soldiers in a sort of self-initiated public relations effort.

Photos like this one, with its accompanying caption information, often made it back to the soldiers' hometown newspapers. Combat photographers were right there, alongside the troops in the field, sharing the same mud, leaky tents, and C-rations. (*Photo by Sp.4 Jacob Hawes, USA Special Photo Detachment, Pacific*)

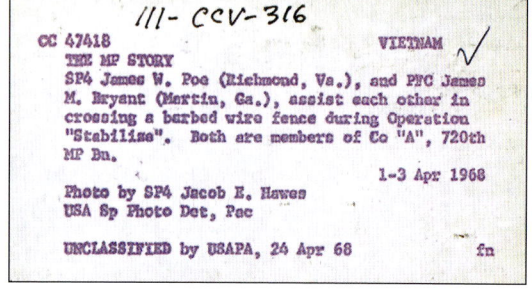

They photographed the everyday activities in and out of combat, the struggles to cope with the conditions in the field, the battles with a mostly unseen enemy, booby traps, helicopter evacuations of the wounded and dead; anything and everything that went on in the war.

Often, when they showed up in the field to cover a combat operation, they would be greeted with shouts of "Hey! You gonna get me in the papers!" (Or *Life* magazine, or on TV, etc.) And often they did. The military saw it as great PR when they could get photos of the troops for their hometown newspapers.

Willy "Wild Bill" Muchler who wrote his story entitled *An Angel on My Shoulder* for this book, said during a TV interview about the book, "When we got out there and took their pictures, it was like somebody really cared about them."

They not only cared and took their pictures, they slogged through the same mud with them, ate the same C-rations, and wept over lost comrades. And sometimes they too were killed in combat, just like their brothers in arms.

The stories in this book are told by the military personnel that lived life in the field, behind the cameras, or in other cases as photo lab technician, or "lab rats." I also became somewhat of an "archivist" and managed to squirrel away hundreds of copies of the prints I and my fellow lab rats made, and managed to bring them home, where today they sit in numerous boxes. Most of the photographers also managed to bring back personal shots not only of the war, but also their views of a country and culture, so new, so strange, so fascinating to them. We've included some of their best shots: kids at play, street scenes from villages and cities like Saigon with its beautiful parks, museums, and even a zoo. After all, the place was not just a war – it was also a country, a culture, and people – a simple fact that is often overlooked when one hears the word "Vietnam."

Vignettes

vi•gnette |vin-yet| noun
1 a brief evocative description, account, or episode.
2 a small illustration or portrait photograph that fades into its background without a definite border.

William Muchler
Then
U.S. Army
Combat Photographer
69th Signal Battalion
Photo Team "B"
Cam Ranh Bay
Republic of Vietnam

"This is me, on the left, with Roy 'Mac' McClellan, my shooting partner on many of my missions. We were taking a break from photographing tank crews guarding Highway #1 just after the attack on LZ English in June of '67. We remain good friends and are in touch with each other even today."

Now
Retired
Plymouth, Pennsylvania

An Angel On My Shoulder

William "Wild Bill" Muchler

I guess I should start off by saying that I am a product of the "baby-boom" era. I grew up in the small town of Plymouth, Pennsylvania. It had its fair share of flag waving, parades, and patriotism in the schools and community in general. My family had several generations that served their country in the military. My grandfather spent thirty-eight years in the Army. My father was in the Navy during World War II along with his brother who was in the Army Air Corps. My brother was in Vietnam with the 1st Cavalry as a door gunner on a chopper in 1966. And then there's me – an Army combat photographer in 1967 with the 69th Signal Battalion.

My friend Billie Young and I were called for our pre-draft exams and passed. We then did what most people would say never to do – volunteer for anything. We decided at that point to enlist for three years instead of getting drafted and only serving two. How does that make any sense? It did for us because it gave us the opportunity to choose the type of military job we wanted. And that was to be aerial photographers.

We got our orders and were shipped off to Fort Knox, Kentucky for our Basic training. Little did we know that because we had been promised two weeks leave after Basic, our school would already have started. As a result, they had to hold us over (and give us extra duties) so we could go on our leaves and start our classes at a later date. After leave, it was off to Fort Monmouth, New Jersey.

When we finally got started on our classes, we found that we were in for more than we ever expected. For me, there was more to this school than I could even imagine. I got introduced to several types of cameras along with how to make all the adjustments and settings for each. I also finally got my chance to take photos from a plane. By the way, did I mention that I had never been in

The vintage 4x5 Graflex like the one I tried to shoot aerials with by hanging out of a Piper Cub.

a plane in my life? When I took a look at the plane I was to go up in, I damn near fell over. It was a single-engine two-seater Piper Cub. That alone scared the life out of me. Reluctantly, I put on my parachute and climbed aboard.

The camera they gave me to use was an ancient bellows camera, a 4x5 Graflex. As we climbed, the pilot told me he was going to bank the plane to the left and I was supposed to hang out the window to take my shots, so I wouldn't catch any part of the wing in the picture. As soon as I put the camera out the window, the wind almost took it out of my hands. As if that wasn't bad enough, we hit a wind pocket that sucked the plane down more than just a few feet. But even after all that I experienced on that first flight, I still wanted to fly and shoot pictures.

Being a photographer was not all that I learned. I was also trained to develop the film and print the photos. I had to learn how to use darkroom equipment, mix the chemicals and more, in the event that I had to work in the lab. I actually enjoyed every bit of learning my new job.

In addition to my photo training, I had other regular military duties. We were usually given weekend passes to leave the base, and since I lived close to New Jersey I would go home for the weekend. The problem I had was making it back for "bed-check". You were supposed to be back on base and in your rack (bed) by a certain time on Sunday evening. I would always get caught coming back an hour or two late and would get restricted to the base and receive extra duty for two weeks. Every time I went home for the weekend I got into trouble.

I finished photo school and got my orders to report to Fort Lee, Virginia. I got there early the next morning, checked into my new company and settled in. I was taken to the on-base photo section to get acquainted with my new job and the people I would be working with. Well, once again, it wasn't what I expected. For one thing we were working together with civilians. They had a forty-hour week; our job was 24/7.

I found out that I was to be a base photographer who covered anything significant that took place on the base. I had to shoot sporting events between different units. I did chain of command photos and formal command dinners with officers and their wives. I also had to do most of my own lab work. After a short time they moved me to the ID card department to operate that section, adding even more to my duties.

Then there were also those good-old military duties. They were about the same as any other base with some exceptions. You had to choose one of these: CPR Training (the use of chemical weapons and gas masks), Riot Control Training, or Burial Squad Detail.

I chose the Burial Squad Detail even though I had no experience with it whatsoever. We had to give military funerals to personnel killed in Vietnam. We covered a 250-mile radius, were given TDY (temporary duty) orders and drew extra pay for our travel. The first one I was assigned to, I was a pallbearer. Later I became a rifleman and a

An Angel On My Shoulder 5

The EM (Enlisted Men's) Club at Camp Gaylor. This could be a wild place at times, with the booze flowing and bands playing. A lot of bands toured throughout the country, appearing at clubs like these on the larger, more secure bases.

Vietnamese workers doing some landscaping around the Camp Gaylor sign and memorial plaque.

flag folder. I even tried my hand at being the trumpeter and playing taps. I practiced playing the trumpet as often as I could. I must say I did get quite well at it.

They finally used me as trumpeter on one of the burials. But as soon as the twenty-one-gun salute went off, a woman let out with a chilling scream. I started to play taps pretty well with the exception of a couple of scratchy notes, but my throat filled up and I had a tear in my eye.

It was then that my true feelings about these guys coming back in boxes hit me. That was the last time I played the trumpet. Soon after that experience I typed out my transfer request for Vietnam. My orders came down in November of 1966. I received thirty days leave and six days travel time to get to Oakland, California, the jumping-off point for Vietnam.

When we got to Oakland they packed all of us into a plane hangar to get ready for our flights to Vietnam. What an experience that was.

We ended up on a four-propeller plane instead of a jet, with a steward instead of a stewardess. Then they had to repair one of the props before we even took off, so they had to put us up in a hotel until it was fixed. In the morning they finally boarded us on the plane. We had to stop in Hawaii to repair the prop once again. The next stop was Guam with a little longer layover; this time they put a completely new prop on the plane.

We finally got to Vietnam. When I first got off that plane it was like someone stuck his hand down my throat and just pulled all the good air out. The humidity was horrible. It must have been well over 100 degrees. We were taken to the 90th Replacement Battalion in Long Binh for final assignment.

They must have needed my job skill badly because they didn't waste much time assigning me. I spent about a week at Long Binh and then was sent to the 69th Signal Battalion Headquarters at Camp Gaylor on Tan Son Nhut Airbase. After two or three weeks there, I was shipped up-country to the 69th's Detachment B at Cam Ranh Bay. For some unexplained reason this is where my mind gets a little hazy.

When you arrived at your new unit in Vietnam, you were the lowest man there and it didn't make much of a difference what your rank was. It was only about two weeks earlier that I had turned twenty-one. That made me the oldest enlisted man in my detachment. I still had no idea what was expected of me. I did a lot of listening to the guys who were there before me but I learned that no matter what unit you ended up in there was always somebody that tried to push you to your limit. Mine was a guy named Bill Burleigh.

For some reason he let it be known that his buddy, John Rankin, would always back his play. I went up to Rankin and asked him if he was going to jump in on the excitement if Burleigh and I had it out. Rankin told me no, it was between Burleigh and me. To make a long story short, we went outside, a few blows were traded, and I ended up pinning him to the outside freezer unit where we kept our film and supplies. While I had him pinned, we had a brief discussion, and everything was settled. After that we got along, but were never actual friends, because he always had something to prove to himself.

After a short time, a Specialist 5th Class NCO named DeRidder sent me out on my first mission with Burleigh. I didn't mind because Burleigh had been on other missions before. I found out later when we got out in the jungle that DeRidder told him to make sure he took good care of me. He told him that wherever he went to "make sure Muchler was right with him". Wherever he was, I was to be right behind him. One time Burleigh turned around and I wasn't there. He had the radio operator calling up all the other platoons in the area until he finally found me. That's when he told me what DeRidder's instructions to him were.

Anyway, we ended on this hill overlooking this dried up rice paddy. Beyond it was a Vietnamese village. We stayed put for some time and then spread out and proceeded to move down the hill and across the open rice paddy. I thought this had to be the dumbest thing I ever saw in my life. We were sitting ducks if the VC opened fire on us.

When we got to the edge of the village there was one portion of the field filled with punji sticks (bamboo stakes with razor edges cut on them that would penetrate right through our boots and into our flesh). By doing that they had made sure that we had to enter the village by the route they wanted us to. Moving through the village was slow because we didn't know what might happen.

Another strange thing that was going on was the fact that there were no civilians in the village at all. Every move you made was scary. There was a trench that lead for about a mile through the village and every few yards there would be a mound of solid ground meant for a machine gun mount. When you walked along the inside of the trench, every so often your feet would hit a piece of wood. It would turn out to be a trap door to an underground tunnel. Then they would call for one of the "tunnel rats" to go down into the tunnel and check it out .

The first time I saw one getting ready to go into the tunnel, I couldn't help but notice he was carrying an M-16 rifle. I had a 45-caliber automatic Colt pistol, and I told him to take it so he could move around better in the tunnel. Fortunately everything did turn out okay and nobody got hurt. I found out later that a couple of days earlier there was a battalion of VC occupying that village and we would have been "lunch meat" for them had they still been there.

On the return back from that mission we were heading toward the landing zone (LZ) to be picked up. I had switched from being with the mortar platoon to accompanying the heavy weapons platoon. About five minutes down the trail, I heard an explosion and we all hit the dirt. Then there was another explosion and then another. There was also quite a bit of screaming.

8   Cameras, Combat and Courage

Burning a suspected Viet Cong village on an operation with the 25th Infantry Division.

An infantryman from the 25th checks and clears a Viet Cong bunker.

A couple of minutes later I heard the MedEvac choppers coming in. The second man in line with the mortar platoon had tripped a wire connected to a couple of hand grenades in a tree, and when they went off it killed the point man. One of the mortars on his back went off killing him too, and wounding the third and fourth guys as well. I quickly learned that even on the trip back after a mission, you had to be alert at all times.

While everything was going on, I was trying to gather and store all this information I needed to stay alive and do my job without thinking about anything else. Later, in the air terminal waiting for my flight back to my unit, I was in a bit of a daze. This would be something that always happened at the end of most of my missions. I do remember that I didn't let on to anyone that I was already having trouble dealing with it all. Some of my reasoning for that was because I didn't want anyone to have to take my place in the jungle and possibly get hurt or killed in my place. I would not have been able to live with that.

One problem was the camera I was given on my first mission. It was YashicaMat 120 twin-lens reflex. You had to open the top and look down into it to take a photograph. Believe me when I tell you that in a combat situation you had to learn to improvise quickly. In my case, I just turned the camera upside down and used it like a periscope.

First mission over, I went back to Detachment B at Cam Ranh Bay. I had to develop my own film and do my own printing. I guessed that everyone wanted to see if I could also handle that part of my job.

After all that, I had to check my notes that I had taken while I was still in the jungle. I kept notes on all of my photos in my book so I knew the names, missions and locations for all of them. What I didn't write down I kept in my head. I would have to say that I knew more details about most of the missions than the average grunt.

Now that I was back at my base camp, I quickly learned that DeRidder had his own plans for me. I think he was planning on training me to take over a lot of his duties while he was away, especially when he found out that I could type and had good office skills. I started typing travel orders for other photographers going out in the field. I was also put in charge of making stencils for captions on photos and keeping a dual set of caption books for all the photos taken by our unit.

I was also trying to readjust to the food in-country. In Vietnam the milk tasted like it was sour. I remember it tasting almost like cream and water mixed. I think it was reconstituted from a powdered form. It was terrible.

I remember my unit having cookouts because we had our own grill, a fifty-gallon drum sliced in half. We used to make deals with the cooks in the mess hall next to our photo office. We would develop film and print photos for them in exchange for cases of chicken and steaks.

Most of the other stuff we needed we had to beg, borrow, steal, or make deals for. The only things we got from our headquarters in Saigon was supplies to make sure we could complete our missions – to photograph the war. If we wanted anything else, we had to scrounge it up ourselves.

We did go down to the village at Cam Ranh Bay as often as we could to unwind. The Vietnamese had a brand of beer called "33", also referred to as "Ba-Me-Ba". The rumor was that "ba-me-ba" was short for embalming fluid. I used to joke around with the guys and tell them not to worry about getting shot because we were all "pre-embalmed" and set to be shipped home. You had to have a warped sense of humor to keep your head on straight.

Over the next couple of months, I went on a few more missions where, for the most part, I was my own boss and watched out for myself. I worked out a routine for myself. If I knew I was going to be gone from the base for several weeks, I would make out extra travel orders and stop over at one of Vietnam's larger cities and spend a day or two and just try to enjoy myself. I thought just in case I did get wounded or anything worse happened it would help take the edge off everything. In my opinion, it did work. I was more relaxed and at the same time I was alert.

In that couple of months I did have a few more memorable things take place. One time, I went out with an armored unit of the 25th Infantry Division. While I was digging in alongside a tank I heard what sounded like a pinging noise. I crawled along the tread of the tank to have a look-see when I saw a piece of dirt fly up in front of my head. A sniper of some sort was trying to harass the crew of the tank. Instead, they almost got me by accident. I saw the turret of the tank turn slightly and then it let loose with a canister round from its cannon. When that happened the tank jumped in the air a few inches. I had never seen anything like that in my life. It scared the hell out of me.

I went back out with this armored unit again a few weeks later. I thought these guys were great. They joked around, had fun, but knew how to do their job. I do remember one thing that happened that was an accident but could have ended up worse than ever. They decided to "drag race" two tanks across an open field to see who could get to the hedgerow first. I was riding on one of the tanks just for the thrill of it all.

When my tank went through the hedges it hit a booby trap that exploded. The impact threw me to the ground. Both tanks stopped dead and everyone looked around. In the meantime I got up, a bit shaken up, and dusted off my ass and got back on the tank. I didn't have a scratch on me. I did have a brush burn on my neck from my camera strap when it swung around.

I never spoke to anyone about anything that happened to me in the jungle. I would only talk about the lighter, even funny stuff that may have happened. Such was the case on the way back from this same mission. We were crossing a dry rice paddy bed with the tanks when I decided to get off and walk for a while.

The Photo Detachment B headquarters building housed our offices and the photo lab. I spent a lot of time there whenever I wasn't out in the field.

What a mistake that was. There was a water buffalo about a hundred yards away. He looked at me, I looked at him, and the next thing I knew he was charging me. I started running away, but he was coming at me like he was on a mission of his own. I could hear some of the other guys laughing. The only thing I figured I could do was shoot at him. While I was running I pulled my 45 automatic out and fired at him.

Luckily for both of us, he stopped in his tracks. I caught up to one of the tanks and jumped on. What a crazy experience. Later, I thought about what it would have been like if my family had received a letter from the Army saying that I got killed by a water buffalo while on a search and destroy mission.

Another mission completed, it was back to Cam Ranh Bay. I recall that when I got back, one of the lab techs took care of my lab chores for me. I was thankful, since I was dead tired. I remember seeing a crate sitting on the floor, but I didn't think it was any of my concern. The next day I found out differently. DeRidder told me to check out the contents of it and let him know what it was.

I opened it up and there were training films in it. DeRidder told me we were going to start a Pictorial and Audio-Visual section there, and it was going to be my responsibility to get it going. After I found out there was no paperwork in the crate to tell me what any of the films were about, DeRidder had me review all of the films and write a brief synopsis of each. When I finished that, I had to make up a stencil for the

I had just jumped up on this tank (I'm the last one on the left) when they decided to "drag race" another tank to a nearby hedgerow. When it hit the hedgerow it triggered a booby trap. The explosion threw me to the ground but I wasn't injured, just shaken up. Later, when I got off the tank to walk for a while, a water buffalo started chasing me, to everyone's amusement.

> *"What a crazy experience!*
> *Later, I thought about what it would have been like*
> *if my family had received a letter from the Army*
> *saying that I got killed by a water buffalo*
> *while on a search-and-destroy mission!"*

movies in numerical order and run off about fifty copies. We had also received three movie projectors and I was told to read the manual on them and get ready to check them and the movies out to the other units on our base.

On top of that, I still had to take care of all the captioning of the photos. I also had to show someone how to do all of my work while I was in the field so it wouldn't be all backed up when I returned. It took me about a week and a half to do that, and then it was time to get my stuff together for the jungle again.

Once again I was back in the air terminal. I decided to go north and stop over in Qui Nhon for the night. That way, another photographer, "Mac" McClellan, who was now my mission partner, and I could go out in the city and relax a bit. Whenever we did that, we had to check our guns at the military police station, which we did here in Qui Nhon. It wasn't too much longer before we wished we had been able to keep our guns.

The POL area (gasoline dumps) at the harbor suddenly went up in a blaze. It was one big explosion. We saw three guys running into the alley across the street from us with five Vietnamese cops chasing them. We heard some shooting. Soon after, the cops dragged the guys out of the alley. We figured it was about time to go to the MP station and tell them we were leaving town and get our guns back. We actually didn't leave town; we went back to the hotel and hid our guns under our pillows.

The next day we heard about a fierce battle going on at a place called LZ English. Soon, we were the only ones trying to get to this place. The MedEvac choppers were bringing guys out of there non-stop. None of them at all would give us a lift. I think they thought we were nuts. We ended up with a tank crew that was guarding Highway #1. They were a nice bunch of guys but we only stayed about two days.

When nothing was going on, I would take shots of the guys doing things like cleaning weapons, eating chow, or pulling vehicles over and checking them out. When they asked me about the pictures I took of them, I told them that it was possible they might be sent home to their hometown papers. I was told that that did happen sometimes. The guys were thrilled to hear stuff like that. We were somewhat like morale builders to these guys.

Mac and I walked along Highway #1 taking photos like a couple of sightseers. For some reason I can't remember much else about it. Forty years later when I looked up Mac, I asked him about it. He told me that two MPs picked us up in a jeep and drove us back to the air terminal.

We got back to our detachment where it was always relatively safe. I tried to catch up on my mail. One of my letters turned out to be quite a shocker. I guess it was what you would call a "dear john" letter. My wife had written and told me she was with someone else and I didn't matter to her anymore.

I immediately got a pass to go to the village and get toasted, drunk, or whatever you want to call it. When I didn't come back for quite a while, Mac and another shooter, Rennie Stafford, came down to the village to pick up the pieces of what was left of me. Since the village closed at 7 P.M. they had to get permission from the MPs to enter. The MPs knew our unit, so they gave them permission to find me. They found me in the part of the village that was off-limits to soldiers and took me back to our hootch.

For a couple of weeks those guys took care of me, covered my job for me, and kept me out of trouble. That's the type of close-knit guys we became. There weren't that many guys in our unit, and we needed to look out for each other. After that slight interruption in my tour of duty I was ready to go back into the jungle again.

The next mission I went on was one that haunts me to this day. I ended up with a company of the 25th Infantry Division. Before I got on the chopper a sergeant asked

14 Cameras, Combat and Courage

Here I am on a tank again. Mac and I were with a crew that was guarding Highway #1 during the attack on LZ English in June of 1967. (*Photo by SP4 Roy "Mac" McClellan, Photo Team B, 69th Sig. Bn.*)

me if I had a gas mask. Of course I told him no. Generally, we weren't issued one. He left and quickly returned and handed me one. Now you have to remember that this was 1967 and we were supposedly not using any chemical weapons at all.

Pilots from the 1st Cavalry were flying us in to our destination. When it came time to drop us off, these guys didn't even land the choppers. They came in at about ten to fifteen feet off the ground and told everyone to jump out the doors. I didn't know this, so I followed everybody else's lead. I ended up in a rice paddy with mud up to my knees and water almost up to my chest. I was holding my camera and gun in the air to keep them dry while I pulled myself out of the muck and climbed up onto a dike.

We made it to the village and I was taking my pictures as usual when someone yelled, "Fire in the hole!" and another one yelled, "Gas!" I put my mask on and continued to take photos. I could hear women and kids screaming and crying. Our guys were using tear gas. I couldn't understand why. We hadn't met any resistance at all.

I knew I had somehow managed to take some good pictures. When I got back to the base unit, I told Lieutenant Duffy, our officer-in-charge, what I had on film and how it affected me. Right off the top of his head he said, "Destroy all the negatives and

One of the bars in the village at Cam Ranh Bay. After getting that "Dear John" letter from my wife I probably hit this one and several others before Mac and Stafford came looking for my lost and by then well-toasted ass and dragged me back to the detachment.

16 *Cameras, Combat and Courage*

**"The next mission I went on
was one that haunts me to this day."**

photos from that mission." I got into a heated discussion with him over that and was later thankful that I hadn't gotten court-martialed for it. Before all of my photos got destroyed, I did make a couple of pictures for some of the guys in my unit including myself. I wasn't the same person after that mission.

The next thing I knew, it was September and I was going to Tokyo on R&R (Rest and Relaxation) for one whole week. It turned out to be a great time. As a fan of shooting pool, I even bought myself a neat three-piece cue stick for when I got back home.

I returned from R&R, and it was off to the jungle once again. This time DeRidder picked me to go with him. I felt good because I liked working with him in the office. When we left I had no idea where we were going.

I found out later that we were joining up with a reconnaissance unit. When we were all set up at the base camp, DeRidder informed me he was going out with a seven-man patrol. He told me not to be worried because it would be safer there in the base camp.

One of the choppers supporting the mission with the 25th Infantry where they went in and tear-gassed a village. Women and children were crying and screaming everywhere. I was never the same person after that mission.

"Home Sweet Home." The tent on the right was our "hootch" that we lived in whenever we were back at our unit's home in Cam Ranh Bay. We even had a doghouse for our team mascot, a mutt the guys picked up somewhere.

I found out that we were in the Mekong Delta and DeRidder was heading for the foot of Black Virgin Mountain.

I crawled under my lean-to, two sticks with a poncho over them. Our unit was firing mortars outside the perimeter at the enemy and I went to sleep. It wasn't too much later when I woke up to explosions all over the place. There were no lights and no moon out and you could see the flashes around us. I rolled over into my foxhole and kept popping up and down taking photos.

That had to be one of the longest nights I ever spent in my tour. When it was light out, we checked the damages. It wasn't all that bad. Then I took a look at my lean-to. The poncho had a hole in it. A mortar round had landed right behind my lean-to and a piece of shrapnel went through the poncho. I was more than lucky.

When DeRidder came back, he saw what had happened and decided we should pack up and head back. I think he was more afraid for my safety than anything else. I can honestly say that I was really happy to be going back to Cam Ranh Bay this time.

When we finally got back, I realized that in all the excitement of that night with all that was happening, I had adjusted the f-stop on my camera wrongly. A lot of my photos did not come out at all. I was furious with myself.

Jenkins took this shot of our 69th Signal Battalion Photo Detachment B (alias, "The Keystone Cops") at Cam Ranh Bay in May of '67. I'm standing in the back, second from the right.

It was at that time that I realized that I was having too many close calls. I was now also considered to be a "short-timer" (under a hundred days to go in-country before leaving for home).

I caught up on the backlog of work in the office that awaited me when I returned. The one other thing I did do, was go up north for a bit, to a place called Da Lat. It was a really nice city. I did some photo coverage of a boat crew that went up and down the nearby river checking out other boats or anything unusual along the shoreline. It was a good cruise and nothing exceptional happened. When I finished there I went into the city, had a good meal and found a soft bed to lay on. I can say I did like that assignment.

From October to mid-November of 1967, Mac and I were both constantly nagged to extend our tour in Vietnam for another six months. They finally made Mac an offer he couldn't refuse, but as far as I was concerned, I was ending my three-year enlistment from the Army right there.

One of the biggest problems at that time was that they didn't have anybody to replace us. It was especially true in my case. With all they had put on me to do, they just couldn't get anyone quickly enough. I gave one guy, Jenkins, a crash course on everything I had to do.

As it got down to my last month, I often would get somewhat uptight. I would think back to the times we were in the jungle when it would be 105 degrees by noon or the times we were there when the monsoon season hit and it would rain day and night for a week or two nonstop. All those times were finally behind me, or so it seemed. December rolled on by and at last my orders came down. I couldn't believe my eyes; the Army was cutting me a break and sending me home a week early.

I'm sure there are some things I've left out of this tale, some that I have stuck way in the back of my head. There's also those things that I can only share with other soldiers and combat photographers that went through the same experiences.

One thing I can share, is that I do not believe we were ever appreciated by anyone other than the men we served with. We didn't get any medals or commendations because we were never actually assigned to the units we served with on all those missions. We picked them; they didn't pick us. That was how we did our jobs. Unfortunately for us, we will live with all that we ever saw and did over there until the day we die. Those of us that were lucky enough to come home, anyway.

I hope you can see now why I entitled my chapter, "An Angel On My Shoulder".

One of the many shops in the village at Cam Ranh Bay. As small and primitive as it seemed, I always looked forward to visiting the village during my time off. This shot was taken by my buddy and "Lab Rat" PFC Dan Brookes.

Roy McClellan
Then
U.S. Army
Combat Photographer
69th Signal Battalion
Photo Team "B"
Cam Ranh Bay
221st Signal Company
Long Binh
Republic of Vietnam

"Here I am at the Photo Section in Cam Ranh Bay. I was probably on front desk duty."

Now
Retired
Flinton, Pennsylvania

Unforgettable Experience – Unforgettable Brothers

Roy "Mac" McClellan

I was born in a small town in western Pennsylvania. I grew up there and graduated from Reade Township High School in May of 1965. I wanted to enlist in the Army then, but my parents would not sign for me. I was only seventeen years old, so I had to wait until I was eighteen.

I enlisted on February 13, 1966, and was promptly shipped to Fort Benning, Georgia for Basic training. I was about to start a part of my life that I knew nothing about or what to expect. Like most other guys who went into the Army, I was going to learn fast.

I made it through Basic and was promoted to Private E-2 when I graduated. I was to go on leave for two weeks then report to Fort Monmouth, New Jersey, for still photography school. We were assigned the oldest barracks on the post, but I got through all right and graduated.

My entire class received orders for Vietnam and had to undergo physical and dental checkups. I could not ship out with my class. I was held over for ninety days for dental work, so I pulled KP (mess hall duty) and worked in the supply room. After they fixed me up I was ready to go. I got thirty days leave and went home. I had to be in Oakland, California on December 26 so at least I was home for Christmas.

I got to Oakland and they processed me in a matter of hours and threw me on a plane for 'Nam. I landed at Tan Son Nhut air base in Saigon at 2 a.m. on December 28. The first thing that impressed me about Vietnam came when I stepped out the door of the plane and literally got stopped by the heat and humidity. I knew right then I was not going to like this, but I asked for it and I had better learn to like it.

We were loaded on a truck and taken to a place they called Camp Alpha with very dusty and smelly screened-in barracks, or "hootches" and told to try and get some sleep and be sure to use the mosquito netting. I found a bunk and tried to lie down and get some sleep, but it just didn't happen. I was lying there thinking about what was going to happen to me when flares started going off. In the light of the flares, I looked up at the two-by-fours that were around the hootch to hold the screens and saw the biggest rat I have ever laid eyes on. It was calmly walking along like it owned the place. Maybe it did.

The next morning they got us up and loaded us on trucks and off we went to Long Binh where we started to process. We were told we would be sent to our unit soon, but would pull details until we were. I ended up pulling perimeter guard in a bunker twice a day. I thought it pretty foolish that all they gave us were three flares and a night stick. They must have thought we could beat the enemy to death. I was in Long Binh for three days, and then they finally called my name and put me on a truck to Camp Gaylor, back at Tan Son Nhut.

I arrived at Headquarters Company, 69th Signal Battalion, and reported to the orderly room. The first sergeant came out and told me I had to report to the CO (Commanding Officer). The CO told me then and there my journey was not over yet. He said that they didn't even have a bed for me and I could go to one of the three detachments they had. I had to choose between Can Tho, An Khe, or Cam Ranh Bay. I knew that Rennie Stafford, a guy I went to photo school with, was in Cam Ranh Bay so I said I would go there. He okayed it and the first sergeant got me some travel orders, a phone number, and a ride to the air terminal and sent me on my way.

When I arrived in Cam Ranh Bay, I made a call and was told to sit tight and someone would pick me up. They did about an hour later. I got to the section and reported in

Just outside the main gate at Tan Son Nhut air base, my first stop in 'Nam. (*Photo by PFC Curtis Hicks, Photo Team B, 69th Sig. Bn.*)

LAYING CABLE—Members of Company B, 40th Signal Battalion at Cam Rahn Bay, use a double mule truck to lay two cables simultaneously in a trench. During the past year, brigade cable units have installed more than 1.4 million feet of cable for radio and telecommunications in Vietnam.
(Photo by Roy A. McClellan, 69th SIG BN)

One of my first photos in Vietnam, the 40th Signal Battalion laying underground cables for communications. Most people knew that this was the kind of thing the Army Signal Corps did, but weren't aware of the fact that we, as photo personnel, were also part of the Signal Corps. It was published in my hometown newspaper, *The Altoona Mirror*.

Rennie Stafford, my buddy from photo school, loading his camera on board a jump plane at a paratrooper training school at Cam Ranh Bay.

to Lieutenant Duffy, who turned me over to Staff Sergeant Habiger. He told me the do's and don'ts of the section and sent me up to the hootches – the two tents where we all would live. I picked a bunk and started trying to unpack in the heat. I would meet every one else later as some guys were in the field. When I did meet them, I got an idea of what I would be into.

The next day, I took my first photos in Vietnam. It was the 40th Signal Battalion laying underground communications cable.

For the next three months I worked in Cam Ranh Bay and took only PIO (Public Information Office) photos – promotions, change of command, and a lot of damaged cargo on the ships in the bay. I didn't get much free time because most of the other photographers were in the field.

After about three months, Sergeant Habiger called me into the office with Rennie Stafford and told him to take me to the field and "show me the ropes." I worked with Rennie from that point on until he went home.

Now comes the hard part of this story.

We would fly out, heading for a certain unit, and sometimes we didn't even know where we were or who we were with. I think my first field trip with Stafford was when we flew to Qui Nhon and caught a chopper up to LZ (Landing Zone) English to the 3rd Brigade of the 25th Infantry. From there we flew to join a unit already in the field. I have no idea to this day where we were. We stayed with them for about ten days, but we did not see any action.

We then went out with another company involved in a pincer sweep trying to move the enemy ahead of them into another company. We walked for three days near the coast and finally on the third night we climbed a hill just to spend the night on high ground. Stafford and I set up for the night and tried to sleep. About an hour after we laid down, the sky opened up and it poured all night. Have you ever tried to sleep with cold water running through your bed? We did not get any sleep that night.

The next morning we got up, rolled up all our wet gear, and packed up to move out. We came down off that hill and split up. Stafford went with one unit and I went with another. We started across a large open rice paddy area about 300 yards wide. The enemy had waited until we were in the middle. I looked down and noticed a lot of little splashes in the water. It did not register in my mind what they were until someone yelled "Hit the dirt!"

We were under fire and I grabbed my camera to take some shots. Some guy yelled get down and yanked me down onto my back in about thirty inches of water, cameras, gear, and all. I wasn't yet even dry from the night before. I am sure he thought he was doing me a favor, but I was just trying to do my job. He had ruined the rest of my day and what film I had in my cameras. We fired back about a thousand rounds of ammo and jumped up and ran into the valley on the other side of the rice paddies.

We found one villager hit in the leg. The medics treated her wound, and we started to sweep the village. A guy who was about 6′4″ and probably 250 or 275 pounds came up beside me and threw a grenade in a bunker. When it went off, I heard a thump and looked at him and he was falling backwards to the ground.

I thought he had been shot because there was blood on the center of his shirt. It turned out to be a piece of shrapnel from his own grenade that came out through the side of the bunker and hit him about two feet from me. I called for a medic, but he was dead when they got there. I helped load him on a medevac (medical evacuation) chopper.

I then helped clear the rest of the village. We found NVA (North Vietnamese Army) flags, medical supplies, and a tunnel the engineers were called in to blow. About then, we heard a lot of firing across the paddies but it did not last long. This was the unit Stafford was with. He told me later that they had killed two VC (Viet Cong) over there.

We joined up again and the CO said they were going to be picked up and flown back to base. We also went back.

By this time we had been out for over two weeks, so we headed back to the section that I dreaded because I knew I would spend the next few days trying to write up captions with my one-finger typing skills.

Such was my first trip to the field, but it was good to get back and get a good shower and clean, dry clothes and boots. It took me an entire day to clean my cameras and my weapon.

Our NCOIC (non-commissioned officer in charge) informed us we would have to stay in the sections for a while because all the other photographers were either in the field or going out. So we were to take PIO jobs and anything else that came up. After a few days the MPs (Military Police) came and asked for a photographer for a job. They did not say what it was, but I was the only one available, so I went.

It was one of the worst jobs I ever had to shoot. It was a suicide of a young guy who had been in-country for about a week. He had put an M-14 rifle in his mouth and pulled the trigger. What a mess. I thought I was going to be sick, but held it down, did my job and got out of there. I was then informed by CID (Criminal Investigations

Dragon Mountain, behind Camp Enari, the 4th Infantry's base camp near Pleiku. (*Photo by Col. Darrell Peck, Staff Judge Advocate of the 4th Infantry Division, March 1969*)

26   *Cameras, Combat and Courage*

A tank emerges from a village road. The armored division was accompanying a mine-clearing operation. Almost as quickly as mines were cleared, they'd be replaced with new ones by the enemy.

A bulldozer razes a sugar cane field while an APC (Armored Personnel Carrier) and infantry provide cover.

Command) that I was not to mention this to anyone. American soldiers do not commit suicide. That's the way it went for two or three weeks, before the other guys came back.

Finally, they gave us orders and we packed up and left for Pleiku and the 4th Infantry base on Dragon Mountain. That was not a pleasant place and I felt bad for the guys who had to be there.

After spending the night, we hooked with a unit going out on an S&D (Search and Destroy) mission, and spent the next week beating the bush and finding nothing but mosquitoes.

We were back and forth for several more trips for the next couple of months and always seemed to be in the right place at the wrong time. It was always "you should have been here last week when we really got into a good fight" or after we left we would hear about the unit we were just with getting hit.

By then it was time for Stafford to go home, so they didn't send him out anymore. I got a new partner, William R. Muchler (Willy). We got along great just like Stafford and I and this made things a lot easier.

We got travel orders and set out for LZ English. We flew to Qui Nhon and we were in the air terminal for three days trying to catch a ride to the LZ. Nothing was going there except ammo, water, food, and replacements. So being young, brave, and stupid, we decided to walk.

We walked all day and at about dusk we were trying to find a place to sleep. Suddenly an MP Jeep came roaring up Highway One. They stopped and a sergeant asked us "Just what in the hell do you guys think you are doing out here?" We explained that we were trying to get up to LZ English. He said "Don't you know they ambushed a convoy along here last week?" Then it was "Get your asses in this jeep and go up with us."

We finally got to English and reported in to the PIO tent. They told us to get something to eat and get some sleep.

The next morning we asked if we could go out with a unit. They told us that there was a large operation with the last, but he didn't know if we could get out with the resupply choppers or not. We would have to try our luck. We hung around the chopper pads all day trying to get a ride out and finally late in the day things started picking up.

I knew by what they were taking that something was happening. I tried almost every chopper and they wouldn't take even one of us because they had the maximum load with food, water, and ammunition. Finally, I went over to a chopper when it was just about dark and asked for a ride. The pilot said he was the last chopper of the day, and I showed him my photo ID thinking that might work. He looked at it, smiled, and said "Son, there is hell out there and I won't take you out to get killed." That was the end of it for the day.

We spent a night at a fire base near the Cambodian border. It was so hot we slept on top of the medics' bunker. About midnight, an entire battery of 8-inch Howitzers like this one opened up, firing right over our heads. The blasts were the only moving air I felt the whole time we were there.

The next day we tried, but couldn't get out to that area. We did get a ride north to another unit, and as usual nothing was going on with them. For two weeks, we beat the bushes and finally used up a lot of film; but there was no action other than the ever present snipers and booby traps. We went back to the section.

Stafford talked the NCOIC into letting him go out one more time before he went home. Staff Sergeant Habiger told him if he got killed not to come back. It wasn't as funny as he intended it to be.

We flew up to Pleiku and got a lift out to a fire base near the Cambodian border. It was just a hole in the jungle; no air could get to you because of the surrounding two-hundred-foot trees even if the wind was blowing. It was a battery of 8-inch Howitzers and a company of infantry. We found a place to set up at the medics' bunker. As usual, we were told "you should have been here …" This did us no good at all, so we took shots of everything we could and a lot of PIO stuff for the unit. It was too hot to sleep in the bunkers so we slept on top. About midnight, the entire battery opened up, firing right over our heads. The blasts were the only moving air I felt the whole time we were there.

*"I showed him my photo ID thinking that might work.
He looked at it, smiled, and said
'Son, there is hell out there
and I won't take you out to get killed.'"*

The next morning there was a patrol going out and we flipped for it and Stafford went out. When he came back, he looked like he fell in a river because he was so soaked with sweat. It was that hot and humid. I had taken the usual shots of the base while waiting for him to get back. When he told me that they had been to a place where a patrol had been wiped out only weeks earlier, I was glad it hadn't happened that day. We had been there for five days and nothing happened except the 4-deuce (4.2) mortar crew had gotten some bad ammo and called in an EOD (Explosive Ordnance Disposal) team to blow it up. I shot that and then we decided to catch a lift out with them.

So it was back to the section and more jobs to shoot back there. One Sunday, SP4 (Specialist 4th Class) Bill Burleigh and I went to the Sixth Convalescent Hospital to shoot a bunch of medal awards to guys who had been wounded and were recovering there.

About this time, I was writing captions at the section and the MPs came by and asked for a photographer. I was next in line, so I grabbed my gear and went with them. I wish I wouldn't have; it was another suicide. It was some young kid who had only been in-country for a week. He put a .45 in his mouth and pulled the trigger. "What a mess," I thought. I choked down my lunch and did my job. It was such a sad feeling to see a young boy wasted like that. I had seen quite a few battle casualties, but this was different. It still bothers me to this day. I guess that is what PTSD is all about.

After I got my captions finished, Muchler and I headed north again. We went to Qui Nhon and tried to get a chopper out with no luck. We were told a convoy was going up to LZ English to the 3rd Brigade of the 25th Infantry and we could catch a lift with them. So we got rooms at the American hotel and went to bed. About midnight, there was some racket in the street and a Vietnamese Police jeep came roaring up the street and stopped in front of the hotel and fired down an alley with the M-60 machine gun mounted on the jeep. Then they jumped out, ran down the alley, and fired a few more shots before they came back dragging two bodies. We went up on the roof to see if we could see anything happening and the sky was all lit up. We were told the next day that they had blown up the ammo dumps. I didn't know if it was the two guys the "White Mice" (what the Vietnamese Police were often referred to as) killed or not. I never found out.

We caught the convoy and rode up to LZ English. We got a chance to go out with an armored unit. It was fun because I had never been on a tank before. We joined an infantry unit for a sweep and didn't find anything. It seemed they didn't want to mess with tanks.

We were going into a village and a young sergeant tripped a mine. It just about blew him in half. I can still see his face. He had been carrying mortar rounds and the rice straw was burning. The rounds were cooking off so we could not get to him for quite a while. Then they swept the village, but didn't find anything else. That night, the tank

30   *Cameras, Combat and Courage*

A 25th Infantry crew fires a "four-deuce" or 4.2-inch mortar. I caught the very tip of the round just as it was coming out of the tube.

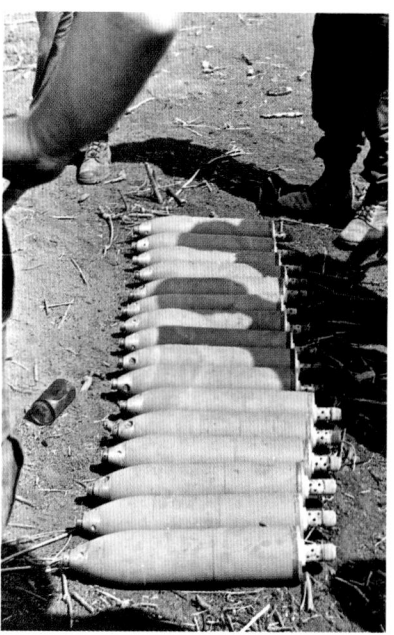

A bad batch of mortar rounds that had to be disposed of.

crew we were with was assigned to watch a bridge. Why, I don't know; there were dry rice paddies on both sides and anybody could have walked right around the bridge. This is the way it went for us. Even when we looked for trouble we couldn't find it. We had been out for two weeks and were running low on film so we went back to the section.

I didn't like the section work much, so I asked to shoot a story about the Special Forces jump school. I spent the next two weeks with the Green Berets shooting that story. It must have turned out pretty good. I got a center page spread in the Pacific Stars & Stripes. I felt pretty good about that and I still do.

Then it was back to the field for me and Muchler. For the next two months it was the same: we got shot at, dodged booby traps, and looked for trouble that we did not find.

It was about then that I decided to extend my tour by six months and got a thirty-day leave. I came back home for the month of December, 1967. I was home for Christmas and then I went back to work.

I got back and settled in just in time for Tet, the Buddhist Lunar New Year at the end of January. We spent that night in a bunker by the hootch. The next morning we all went to the section and geared up to go to the field, but I got a job to shoot damage at the air base. It seemed that the NVA had fired from across the bay and hit three C-130

Unforgettable Experiences – Unforgettable Brothers   *31*

aircraft. They did a good job on them. I was there for hours.

I got back and continued to get ready to go to the field, but I was told I had a job that would take weeks to shoot. I would not be going to the field. The CO of II Corps wanted color slide shots of all the damage caused during the attacks, and anyway I was ill. So I spent the better part of a month flying all over II Corps, shooting all the damage – and there was a lot. I shot about 7,000 color slides. This was my luck, good or bad, such as it was.

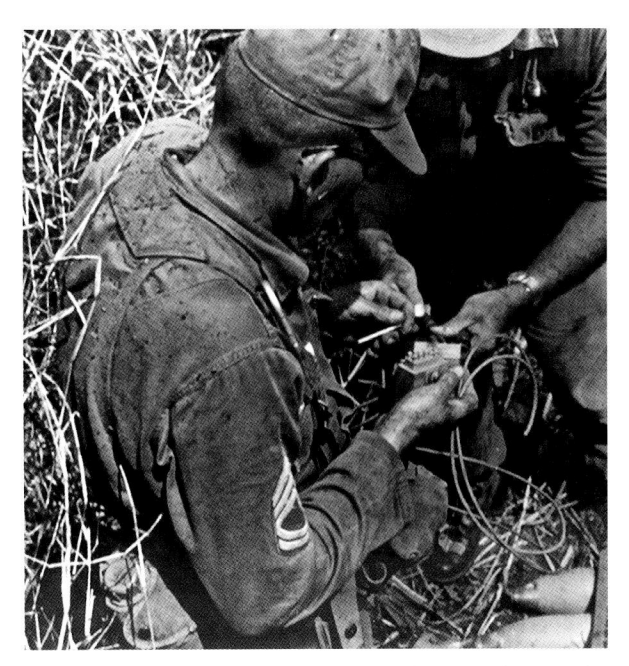

An EOD (Explosive Ordnance Disposal) team wires up the explosives to blow up the batch of defective mortar ammo.

I later learned that our unit had lost nine photographers during Tet. By this time, we had been transferred to the 221st Signal Company, a complete photography unit stationed in Long Binh.

I had been promoted to E-5 and by this time and was ranking NCO in the section. I had to spend more time at the section, so I could not go to the field as much. Everyone had gone home and we had all new people to train.

My time was running out so I typed myself some travel orders and went to the field. I headed north to the Central Highlands that was our area. I got hooked up with a unit going out for what they called an extended patrol. Was it even! As usual, I had no idea where I was or who I was with, but we kept going, day after day. We were out for over three weeks in the jungle and were resupplied by chopper when we needed it. We had several fire fights and it seemed like we were chasing the same enemy unit over and over. When we caught up to them, we fought.

It was in one of these fire fights that I killed my first enemy soldier. They were breaking off and he stood up to leave and I shot him in the chest with an M-1 carbine that I had traded for with a Green Beret. I can still see the look on his face. Like what happened, it was very odd. We had a couple of wounded and they were medevacked out and we kept going. I killed one more on that trip and finally found the answer to what I had wanted to know for over a year – whether I could do it or not.

We finally came out of the jungle into a very large paddy area that was dry. There they had set up hot showers and had hot food waiting for us: steak, potatoes, beans –

and green hot dogs. I swear they were green as grass, but they tasted pretty good after over three weeks on C-rats (C-rations).

They told us to strip down and shower and they handed out new fatigues. I was glad for that because mine were rotting and all torn. They doused them with gas and burned them to make a nice fire in the hundred-degree heat. By the time we were all done, the choppers were coming in to pick us up and take us back to Pleiku, Dragon Mountain, home of the 4th Infantry. From there, I went back to the section because I was out of film anyway.

As soon as I got there, the CO called me into his office and read me the riot act because I had written my own orders and went to the field while he was in Saigon. Shortly after that, I extended again. However, it was only three months this time, because that was all the longer they would let me stay. So I settled into being NCOIC and running the section. I didn't shoot any jobs; I just ran the office and assigned work. But we were getting short on people. We were not getting any replacements. I talked the CO into letting me go out in the field one more time.

I went north and hooked up with a unit of the 7th Cavalry. As usual, I had no idea where we were. It was pretty heavy jungle and it was tough going. We ran into an ambush on the second day.

It's hard to describe a fire fight: noise, yelling, and the buzz of bullets going by. It is very unnerving, but you do the best you can. The grunts had more experience and handled it better than me.

It was during this chaos that I shot a third enemy soldier. I have never told anyone about these three soldiers. I always thought it was nobody's business but mine. I told the VA (Veterans' Administration) psychologist about the first one, but not the other two. I think it is time to tell about it now, because we are trying to explain in this book just what we went through over there. It wasn't easy then and it's not easy to tell now.

We had several wounded and medevaced them. Because of this, we headed back to base.

General Gates and some admiral. Our section was right across the street from II Corps Headquarters, so they were always bugging us to take these "grip & grin" shots.

I was a little shook up. I think that was the closest I came to getting killed. I still think I was just lucky and God was looking after me.

I came back to the section and spent the rest of my time getting ready to go home. It seemed like a long time, but it was only about a month. I was a "short-timer" and glad of it. After that, I just spent my time training a replacement to run the section.

Finally, my orders came through and I started to pack my gear to come home. I left Vietnam around September 25, 1968.

That's about all there is to tell. When I got to Oakland and processed out, I went to the airport to come home and there were a bunch of hippies standing in the airport. One of them spit on my uniform. I swear I would have killed him, but there was a police officer there and he chased them off. I am proud I served and damned proud of that uniform. I feel I earned the respect we did not get when we came home.

I caught a flight home and ended my service.

I know things are kind of jumbled and out of order, and that I didn't know the names of places where a lot of things happened, but it is the best I can do after forty-five years.

I finally got away from the section to do a story on the Special Forces airborne training or "jump school" at Cam Ranh Bay. These Vietnamese trainees are doing practice jumps from a tower. The story turned out pretty good – I got a center page spread in the *Pacific Stars & Stripes*. I felt pretty good about it then, and I still do.

Me during the shoot at the jump school.

Green Beret Jump School, Cam Ranh Bay

I also know I missed a lot of things that happened. You try for years to forget, and then suddenly you try to remember. It doesn't work too well.

Well, that's about all I can say. After years and years, some of us started to contact each other and that is why I am writing this. I'm trying to explain what we did over there and why I am proud of what I did and what we all did. I feel a lot of pride for all military combat photographers, because we have never received the recognition we deserve. It was an experience I will never forget; nor will I ever forget all my brothers, wherever they are.

Unforgettable Experiences – Unforgettable Brothers   35

After we were fired on from a village, we rounded up everyone for questioning.

VC prisoners being taken back to the base camp. This was somewhere along the coast – the South China Sea is in the background.

36   *Cameras, Combat and Courage*

Photo Detachment B, 69th Signal Battalion, Cam Ranh Bay, June, 1967

Some Photo Detachment B, 69th Signal Battalion members posing in front of our "bar & lounge" area. *Front row, left to right:* John Rankin, ??? Miller, Garland Westberry, Willie Brooks, Marty Barnes, Lieutenant Michael Duffy. *Back row, left to right:* Dan Brookes, James Wright, Bill Burleigh, me, and ?? Thigpen. June 26, 1967.

Unforgettable Experiences – Unforgettable Brothers 37

Curtis D. Hicks (Rose)
Then
U.S. Army
Combat Photographer
69th Signal Battalion
Photo Team "B"
Cam Ranh Bay
Republic of Vietnam

"Checking out my brand new 35mm Asahi Pentax unit! After dragging around a 4x5 press camera on several missions, it was almost like being given a treasure ... THREE lenses, one of them a 70mm-150mm zoom ... Man! I was thrilled!"

Now
Sculptor
Decatur, Indiana

(*Photo courtesy of the* Fort Wayne Journal Gazette)

THE DEATH OF fear

Curtis D. Hicks (Rose)

Beginning to learn to be "… thankful for all things …"
Ephesians 5:20

Editor's note: Curtis has chosen to tell his story in a unique blend of writing style and punctuation, hence referring to himself with a lower case "i" etc.

> *"i could never have guessed that some of the deep-rooted fears that had haunted me in my childhood and tormented me into my adulthood would be totally destroyed by a stray machine-gun slug crashing into my forehead."*

As an only child of a single mom, raised in the stifling atmosphere of an ultra-strict religious movement during the "fifties", i grew into an angry and rebellious young teen. Shortly after turning seventeen, i joined the army (August 1963), fulfilling one of my childhood dreams. The rigors of Basic and Advanced training were disciplined enough for me to feel the comfort of a watchful, masculine eye for the first time in my life; and i actually enjoyed the time there. However, after i was shipped to Germany and assigned regular duty, my old restless spirit and dissatisfactions surfaced again. Drunkenness, lack of respect for authority, and my ability to be "Absent With-Out Leave" for weeks at a time gave me a chance to fulfill my other childhood dream. "Going to prison." (i had been fascinated with prison movies as a child.) After being AWOL for a month, turning myself in, and then going AWOL again while on house arrest, i was immediately court-martialed, reduced to the lowest pay-grade, and sentenced to four months in a military prison. (i later learned many young men that have been cursed with the lack of a good father have an innate longing to be "told what to do", and for the company for other men; possibilities for which the military and prison provide ample opportunities.)

When i was reassigned to Vietnam as a Combat Photographer in September of 1966, the rebellious spirit within me was turned up another notch. i started using drugs a

Sand dune behind our tents with a sandbag bunker built into it. When i first arrived at the Cam Ranh Bay Photo Team B unit, i didn't know anyone else there who smoked pot, so I would go up there each evening to get stoned by myself. After my first evening at the South Beach Chapel, i threw all of my marijuana away, and the bunker became my "Prayer Closet."

day or so after arriving at the reception station in Long Binh. After being assigned to the 69th Signal Battalion at Tan Son Nhut AFB, amphetamines, barbiturates (available without prescription at Vietnamese pharmacies) and marijuana, became part of my daily life. The effects of reading about "hippies" in Life and Look magazines, and the music i was absorbing, rapidly made deep changes in my lifestyle. In a short time, my superiors made an appointment for me with an army psychiatrist. i was only in his office for a few minutes when he cleared me for a mentally unfit discharge. As I was being processed, my platoon sergeant, SFC McMillan, (an even-tempered, generous man) took me aside and said, "Curtis, I hate to see you get a bad discharge. Is there anything we could do to help you get through the rest of your tour here without any further trouble?" i suggested that he try sending me to our detachment at Cam Ranh Bay, where i had several friends that i'd not seen for awhile.

When i got off the plane in Cam Ranh, i was really stoned. Wandering into the 3rd Corp Air Transport Quonset-hut to ask for directions, i saw on the wall behind the counter a cardboard sign that read "Good Gospel Singing, Pentecostal Services," stenciled in a circle, with the time and location printed in the center. In that condition, i thought to myself, "Hey! i'll have to go down there sometime! Maybe i'll meet somebody that knows my mom." Little did i know that GOD would be there waiting for me, and HE was very well acquainted with my mother, in part due to the years she had spent praying so seriously for me.

A few weeks later, i took one of our jeeps to the South Beach Chapel, where fifty or more officers and enlisted men sang songs of worship that i remembered from my

South Beach Chapel in Cam Ranh Bay, the building where i first committed my life to the Lord as an adult.

Left of photo, our shower; it had hot water available until about 30 minutes after sunset, and not again until the sun warmed it up the next morning. Our "party hootch" is in the center and one of our sleeping tents is on the right. It was so "upscale" that it had a wood floor!

i was Baptized in the name of Jesus in the South China Sea in Cam Ranh Bay by Elijah Williams, a drafted Pentecostal Minister from Alabama, one of the best men i have ever known. i have long regretted that at that time in my life, i was too shallow to keep in touch with him.

childhood. One young man from New York City testified about the wonderful changes in his life since he had received the Baptism of the Holy Spirit; (just the week before!) with such a buoyancy and glow that i knew immediately that he had just exactly what i wanted.

i joined a prayer group that met weekly; began to read a New Testament provided by the Chapel, and to memorize favorite Scriptures. i was even Baptized in the Name of Jesus in the South China Sea. But, because of childhood hangovers from

This photo and blow-up insert on the left show the hole left by the .45 caliber slug that REALLY got my attention. Later, one of the guys found it on the floor and gave it to me. i still have it, mounted on this bracelet i often wear.

not understanding God's grace, i still possessed the fearful feeling of not being one of God's own. Those old fears rose up with a vengeance, terrifying me with the possibility of being killed while on a mission before i was able to "dot all the i's and cross all the t's", according to the requirements of the brand of Pentecostalism i had grown up in. i was growing more serious about my relationship with God, but the fear of death and missing out on Heaven continued to dwell in my thoughts; after all, i had not yet "worked out" my own salvation. It was like a recurring dream. As far back as grade school, i had been an easy target for bullies. Too frightened to fight back, i just suffered through the humiliation as best i could. When i

Me writing captions at a desk back in the Camp Gaylor office of the 69th Sig. Bn. at Tan Son Nhut air base in Saigon. My ever-present Salems are close at hand. i smoked them for 15 years. We did not have to go outside to smoke back then. Lot harder quitting them than the mostly psychedelic drugs i also used, but i did "get away" at last.

grew older, the same thing would often happen in a bar or at a party -- as though i had a sign hanging over my head that read, "Hey! Beat this guy up!" Now, i was being bullied and beaten up once again, but this time by an invisible (and far more powerful) foe.

Sitting in a straight-back chair at a desk in our base photo office, i had just finished a letter to my mom. i tilted the chair back with my fingers laced behind my head to stretch a bit, as i lowered the front legs of the chair to the floor, there was a sound like a truck backfire, something hit me in my head and knocked me out into the middle of the room. Jumping back up, i threw my left hand to my forehead and began to run down the long rectangle of the room i was in, toward the exit nearest our bunker, certain that we were under attack. i had not reached the end of the room when i noticed i was the only one running! i turned around and looked down the room through the doorway

> "... there was a sound like a truck backfire, something hit me in my head and knocked me out into the middle of the room. Jumping back up, i threw my left hand to my forehead and began to run down the long rectangle of the room i was in, toward the exit nearest our bunker, certain that we were under attack."

44   *Cameras, Combat and Courage*

THE DEATH OF *fear*   45

"A chance to visit the Cao Đài Temple in Tay Ninh was perhaps the highlight of my short photography career. This opportunity fell into my lap because of the timing of my arrival in Tay Ninh just prior to the beginning of Operation *Junction City* in late February, 1967. The local U.S. Military in charge of the arriving reporters and photographers put together some buses to give us an opportunity to see one of the most important local sites, and the photos i got to take there were always a treasure to me and the most special event of my time as a photographer."

near where i had been sitting, into the front office. Several of the guys were sitting in a circle "shooting the breeze" when i noticed Rennie Stafford, with whom i had gone to photo school, grinning at me, as if my joke was pretty good, but he was the only one who had gotten it. i remember thinking to myself, "Well, i'll show you!" i walked to where he sat, took my hand off my forehead, and the blood began to run down my face. The look on his face was well worth the walk to where he was. The smile went away immediately. i sat down on the floor cross-legged (a position i cannot recall having ever sat in before), never lost consciousness, but for several minutes my mind was like a broken record. Over and over and over again it repeated, "Thank-You-Jesus!–Thank-You-Jesus!-Thank-You-Jesus!"

A short time passed, when the door to our lieutenant's office opened and he stepped out to assess the damage. He and a young second lieutenant (who had just arrived "in country") had been examining a "trophy weapon" that had been captured from the Viet Cong. It was a Thompson 45-caliber drum-feed machine-gun (favored by the gangsters in the movies) which had probably been captured from the French years before. My lieutenant said the "new guy" had placed the weapon on his desk (not realizing that the safety mechanism was set on full cock with a round in the chamber) and the jar of touching the desk released a round, piercing through the wall of his office, through the corner of the developing lab and into the room where i was sitting. Traveling on a slight incline, it ricocheted off the Masonite ceiling, then slammed into my forehead.

We all knew that if i was taken to the base hospital to be checked out for an injury caused by a bullet, there would have to be an investigation, due to the base commander's policy of no one "ever" having a loaded weapon. So, after the bleeding stopped, i was driven to our tent and given the remainder of the day off. i didn't even suffer a headache. Since it was so hot, i walked back to the office and spent the rest of the day there, never again fearing an accident, death, or injury. i was firmly convinced that if God wanted to take care of me, He was perfectly capable of doing so; there was no reason for me to worry any longer.

In the years that followed, i often pondered about my mind's immediate response to the sudden accident. i believe it was God's Spirit within me that prompted my brain to utter the words of thankfulness. Now, as i look back over the years and into my Christian infancy, i can see this was the first step in my journey toward beginning to learn about "Giving thanks always for all things …" (Ephesians 5:20); "In everything give thanks…" (I Thessalonians 5:18); and, "… all things work together for good …" (Romans 8:28). No matter how difficult or painful circumstances may seem to be at the moment, if we are honest in our attempt to live a life pleasing to God, maintaining a Thankful Spirit for God's mercy (which endures forever), will always be a giant step in the right direction.

After i finished my tour at Cam Ranh Bay, i went back to the "World" and finished my enlistment at Fort Riley, Kansas. When i came home, i wanted to have a "Church family" to be a part of, and since i knew nothing about "Christianity" except what i had learned as a child, i gravitated in that direction.

While on my first leave, i met a girl from the Church i had attended as a child, and a year later we got married. Now, the last twenty-three years of my life have been a journey of continued Spiritual Growth, which i am Thankful for everyday. i have not met any other people who have had the experience of escaping from a "religious personality cult" as i have done.

One of the main reasons any man becomes connected to a personality cult, is "growing up without a father". If that happens to you, then You have a subconscious longing for 'someone to tell You what to do.' That is what the military does, that is what prisons do, and that is what religious cults do. My parents were divorced before i was born, and i can still remember as a young child, the only thing i ever really wanted was a Dad. i spent almost six years in the Army, some time in a military prison, and spent time in a personality cult as well.

Sure glad i lived through all three of them!

48 *Cameras, Combat and Courage*

William Mondjack
Then
U.S. Army
Photo Lab Technician
("Lab Rat")
69th Signal Battalion
Tan Son Nhut, Saigon
Republic of Vietnam

"Bob Hillerby took this shot of me at Long Binh on my last day in Vietnam. Soon after, I was at Bien Hoa boarding the "Freedom Bird" to take me home."

Now
Beekeeper
Whitehall, Pennsylvania

My Story – Vietnam 1966–1967

William Mondjack

I grew up in the small village of Hokendauqua, in Whitehall Township, Pennsylvania. I graduated from Whitehall High School in 1964. The summer of '64 was great; I had a job, bought a car and just hung out with my friends. While Dad would watch the news every night and read all the current events in the newspaper, I had no interest in any of it. I heard something on the news about Vietnam but didn't pay much attention to it. My interest was photography.

I can't remember at what age I started taking pictures, but I can remember using a plastic Kodak camera that used 127 roll film. I'd shoot photos of family members and our dog. At about age 15 my Mom bought me a 35mm Yashica; that's when I started shooting Ektachrome. I remember thinking I couldn't afford to buy an enlarger to print my own black and white photos, so the first roll of film I developed was Kodak Ektachrome. It was slide film, so all you had to do was process it, dry it, cut it into individual frames and mount each one in a cardboard holder. After that, you could look at them in a slide viewer, view them on a large screen with a slide projector, or send them out to have color prints made.

It was the winter of 1964-1965 that I met my girlfriend Carol. We spent all of our free time together throughout the whole year of 1965. I also would usually meet a bunch of my friends at a local diner where we would plan our weekends and sometimes arrange to double date.

It was sometime in the autumn of '65 when a couple of us were sitting at the counter in the diner. One of the guys said "Look what I got in the mail today!" and reached into his jacket pocket. He pulled out his draft notice. That got our attention to say the least. As the weeks went by, one by one more of the guys got their draft notices as well. We knew they were going to Vietnam. I knew I did not want to go. I was happy with life the way it was.

Later that year a friend of mine asked me to go along with him to the Post Office – he wanted to enlist in the Army for electronics. I went along with him but had no interest in enlisting. I joined my friend at the enlistment office and after he signed up the big old sergeant asked how he could help me, but I told him I did not want to enlist. He then asked what I was interested in and I answered, "Photography." He said, "We have some fine photography schools, we have still photography, motion picture, and photo lab." My eyes lit up and I said I'd be interested in still photography school but I didn't want to go to Vietnam. He replied, "Oh, you won't go to Vietnam, you'll probably go to Europe." When I returned home, I told my mom and dad I'm thinking of joining the Army to go to photography school. I don't remember them objecting, but I knew they were concerned.

All of my uncles were in WW II; my uncle Bill, whom I was named after, lost his life in that war. One day when my uncle Joe was visiting, I mentioned that I was thinking of joining the Army. I remember him telling me "Don't volunteer for anything and don't be the first in line or the last. Do what you're told and you'll do OK."

It was January of 1966 when I enlisted. I was sent to Fort Jackson, South Carolina, for Basic Training. After Basic I was a "hold over." About 14 of us were held over because we hadn't received our orders for our various schools. I was told my school was full and I would get in on the next class cycle.

The Army does not let you sit around and do nothing; most of the guys were policing up the grounds and painting cigarette butt cans. I had a military driver's license, so I had the job of delivering blocks of ice to all of the mess halls at Fort Jackson for the next two months.

Finally, my orders came through to report to Fort Monmouth, New Jersey. I was notified that I had been transferred into Photo Lab School instead of Still Photography. I was so glad to leave Fort Jackson that I didn't care what school I was going to attend as long as it had to do with photography. I'm not one who had liked school very much, but this I really enjoyed.

A week before graduation we were called out to formation and were told that all the leaves usually given after graduation were cancelled and everyone would ship out directly to their overseas assignment except those going to Vietnam. Those individuals would receive a 30-day leave. We had 31 in our graduating class; 21 were sent to Europe, five to the Panama Canal Zone and five to Vietnam. I was one of those going to Vietnam.

I was still kind of pleased, because I got the 30-day leave and 5 days of travel time to get to California. I spent all of my free time with Carol and my family. Finally, the time came to catch my flight to California. I remember how emotional it was leaving Carol at the airport as I watched her through the plane window. It was September of 1966. I was 20 years old and Carol was 17. As the plane lifted into the air, I wondered if I'd ever see her again.

The flight was impressive. The Braniff Airlines jet was big and bright blue. We were served meals and got to watch a movie. The long flight took about 25 hours, with stops for fuel and food. As we approached Tan Son Nhut Airport, the pilot announced we would be descending rapidly to avoid small arms fire. We did land rather quickly, and when the doors finally opened, the heat and humidity that hit us was a real wake-up. I was in Vietnam.

I believe they bused us from Tan Son Nhut to Long Binh for processing. That's where we got to experience "shit-burning" detail. I think everyone got to do that. We had to drag half of a 50-gallon drum full of shit out from under the latrines, mix it with diesel fuel and burn it off. It was a more than disgusting duty. While at Long Binh my personal camera got damaged and I was unable to take any photos.

Within a few weeks, I was sent to the 69th Signal Battalion at Camp Gaylor on the Tan Son Nhut Airbase. When I arrived I was assigned to the photo lab. About a half dozen of us arrived; I don't remember who else was with me. The camp seemed to be in the process of building Quonset huts and there was no room for us, so the First Sergeant found an empty storage shack where we could sleep. There were no mosquito nets, but at least they found us some cots. I remember waking up the next morning and counting over 100 mosquito bites.

At first we worked six days with one day off until more troops came in. Then our workdays came down to eight hours. I started out printing black and white photos, but

This billboard was somewhere along the road from the replacement camp at Long Binh to Tan Son Nhut. I guess it was to welcome the tourists, but I never saw any and sure as hell didn't feel like one either.

before long I moved into our makeshift color lab and began processing Ektachrome, mostly on the night shift. We did have some problems at first.

One night, I remember processing about 16 rolls of film and during the rinse cycle all of the emulsion floated right off the acetate and down the drain. The next morning the shit hit the fan when a 2nd lieutenant who didn't know shit bitched at me and said I had done it all wrong as he read off the processing instructions. In reality, the dumbass was reading the processing instructions for C-22 color negative film and not the ones for E-3 and E-4 Ektachrome. I wrote a letter to Kodak explaining my dilemma and they sent me instructions for processing in tropical conditions. From then on all went smooth and I processed a lot of personal film for guys in the mess hall, trading my work for ice cream.

Whenever I had time off I would head out and photograph the Vietnamese people. Even though I loved developing Ektachrome I was a photographer at heart. It was fascinating to capture the faces of the old people and children.

Our group of guys in the lab was unique. Most of us had a sense of humor and we all got along. Living together for a year we got to know each other quite well. When we had time off and were not out "shooting" (pictures) we would sometimes exchange stories about our family life back home "in the World." As each one of us got to be a "short-timer" (90 days or less left in-country) we would give each other a sendoff with a handshake and well wishes for a safe trip home. The thing I regret now is I never

Some of the Photo Lab guys at Camp Gaylor. Left to right, Dan Brookes, Willie Brooks, Wheaton, Henry Garcia, Sergei, and me (in civvies). I remember the guy in the front middle as just "Mac." We all had a crazy sense of humor and had a lot of fun together, shooting pictures around Saigon, or just swapping stories about our lives back in the "World."

Silent Night

Christmas Day Dinner
VIETNAM 1966

Shrimp Cocktail
with Cocktail Sauce and Crackers
Roast Tom Turkey
Giblet Gravy
Cornbread Dressing
Snow Flaked Potatoes
Glazed Sweet Potatoes
Cranberry Sauce
Buttered Garden Peas
Crisp Relish Tray
Parkerhouse Rolls
Butter
Pumpkin Pie with Whipped Cream
Mincemeat Pie
Old Fashion Fruit Cake
Fresh Chilled Fruit
Mixed Nuts
Assorted Candy
Tea
Coffee
Milk

The mysterious Christmas Dinner menu. No one that I knew ever remembered having this food on Christmas Day: shrimp cocktail, turkey, "snowflake" potatoes, gravy, cranberry sauce, pies? Maybe it was the Officers' Mess Hall menu.

asked anyone for their address or phone number. It would be nice to get together with some of the guys now.

I used to send pictures home to my parents and Carol. I'd send slides home in envelopes and 8 x 10 and 11 x 14 prints in boxes. The thing that I am most proud of is Carol (my girlfriend) took a box full of my photos to an editor at our local newspaper. She told the editor that her boyfriend was in Vietnam and she thought these photos deserved to be published in the newspaper. One of the editors turned her down but another took a look and decided to publish two full pages of my photos. I received a letter of appreciation, a check, and a job offer from the chief photographer, something I cherish to this day. I just recently had these pages mounted onto wood plaques.

The second memory I value is the fact that Carol and my mom would write me every single day. Some days Carol would write me two letters and put the time on the

54   Cameras, Combat and Courage

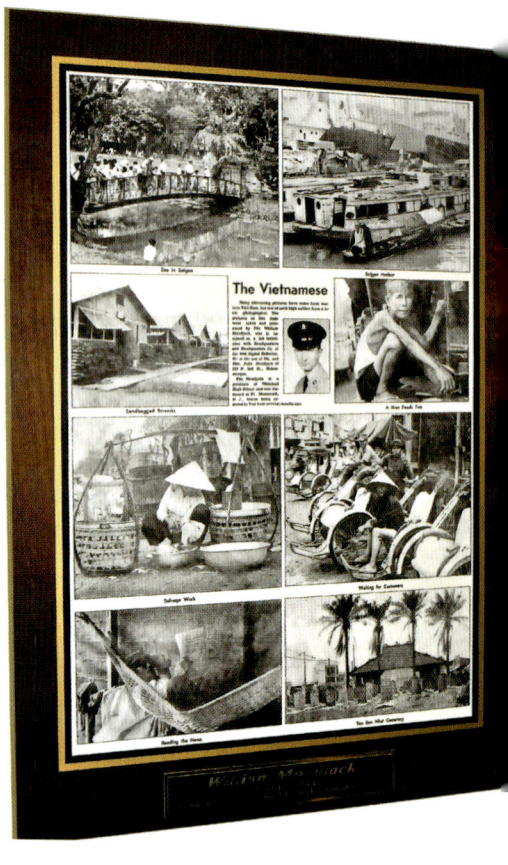

Pages from my local newspaper that published some of my Vietnam photos while I was still there, through the efforts of my girl friend and now wife, Carol. After one editor turned her down, she went to another who gave my photos a two-page spread. I recently had them mounted onto these wooden plaques. I'm pictured with them here on display at the Lehigh Valley Heritage Museum in Allentown, Pennsylvania.

back of the envelope. Wherever I was stationed in the Army, I always received the most mail. No e-mail or Internet in those days, so it took a lot of love to keep those letters coming every day.

Some of my friends left Vietnam for home and got an "early out" of the army because they had 90 days or less left of their military obligation. I had signed up for three years, so I wasn't as lucky. I left Vietnam and returned home in September of 1967 and had 15 months left to serve. I had a 30-day leave before reporting to my next duty station at Fort Lee, Virginia.

My Story – Vietnam 1966–1967 55

A closer look at the plaques.

Flowers for sale on Nguyen Hue Street during the Tet holiday.

Lady navigating a Sampan down the river.

My Story – Vietnam 1966–1967 57

Kids in their village home.

Old man cooking food down by the Saigon River.

Buddhist monks at the National Zoo in Saigon.

Clockwise, from above: Saigon street market; pedal-powered cyclos awaiting customers in Saigon; this Buddhist temple had these giant cones of incense with little calendars attached hanging from the ceiling – I was fortunate that they allowed me inside to take photographs; two schoolgirls taking a break for a snack; two shy little kids peeking out from a doorway.

My Story – Vietnam 1966–1967   59

60   *Cameras, Combat and Courage*

Soldier standing guard on the corner of 7th & N Street NW in Washington D.C. with the ruins of buildings that were destroyed during the riots that followed the assassination of Martin Luther King, Jr. I found myself walking guard duty on the streets of our nation's capital. Soldiers were pulled from all the nearby bases and sent to D.C. for riot control. All of a sudden, the public appreciated us, unlike when we first returned from Vietnam. (*Photo from the U.S. Library of Congress*)

I thoroughly enjoyed my 30 days home and almost totally forgot Nam, but that leave went by too fast for me. When I got to Fort Lee, it was back to military life, living in the barracks with a bunch of guys I didn't know, inspections, formations, extra duties – and I really missed Carol. I would go home on weekends when I could, but going back to the barracks really sucked. So sometime in January of 1968 we decided to get married. Carol did all of the planning for the wedding to take place in April.

I guess it was around March when I put in for a leave but come April, Martin Luther King was assassinated and riots broke out in Washington, D.C. They pulled almost everyone they could out of Fort Lee and put us on riot control in D.C. I found myself walking guard duty on the streets of our nation's capital. I don't remember the Army feeding us for quite some time. Fortunately, the Red Cross was there and gave out coffee and donuts. The civilians of the city handed us food while we were walking guard blocks around the city. I had some great meals at some fancy restaurants. We were really appreciated while we were there.

I remember when we pulled into Washington, we must have had 50 or more deuce-and-a-half trucks full of guys, driving though red lights for miles and miles until we stopped at one of the police precincts to unload some of us. The people of the city came out onto the sidewalks and cheered for us. Nothing like the days when we came home from Nam.

It all came to an end just in time for me to come home and marry Carol. After our honeymoon I brought her back to Fort Lee where we rented an apartment off base. It was more like a hunter's cabin back in the woods and very private, but we were just married and it worked out just fine. I got the position of Post Photographer at the Communications Center of Fort Lee and loved my work. I also did fingerprinting and photo ID cards.

One day a major came into the photo section and complimented me on my photography. He told me that he liked how much thought I put into my work. My response was, "I like what I do." He told me if I ever needed a favor I should call on

After Vietnam, I was appointed Post Photographer at Fort Lee, Virginia. This picture ran in the post newspaper with the caption: "SSgt. Aubrey Antone 'bequeaths the tools of his trade, a camera and an official U.S. Photographer's armband, to his successor,' Sp4 William Mondjack, during a farewell ceremony for the sergeant who received his discharge from the Army last week.

Gerald Yanke, another lab guy, and I persuaded a local to take us for a sampan ride down the Saigon River. At first he wouldn't do it, saying it was dangerous. We paid him a few hundred piasters and off we went. Not long afterward someone was shooting at us as we motored down the river. Yanke and I took cover in the bottom of the boat. For some reason at the time we were both laughing about it. I guess we thought it absurd that some sniper would be shooting at two guys in civvies out for a simple boat ride. Shortly after, I got this photo of water buffalo in the river.

him. I thought to myself "What kind of favor would I ever need?" But the offer was nice to hear.

I thought everything was going OK for the both of us until I received a notice to report to the MP (Military Police) Company. It seemed that they desperately needed to replace many MPs that were rotating out of the service and were pulling a draft from each division of the company. I went to see that major and explained my dilemma. He made a call and got me off the orders.

I think it may have been a month or so later that I received orders to return to Vietnam for a second tour. I did not want to go back again so I had to see the major and hope he would grant me a second favor. He said he couldn't promise, but he'd give it a try. Successful once more, he got me off those orders as well. Carol and I stayed at Fort Lee until my discharge in January of 1969.

I originally enlisted for Still Photography and really wanted to go to school for it. I loved what I was doing, but always thought I would have liked to have been a photographer in Vietnam, instead of a photo lab tech. But then maybe, just maybe, I may not have returned home. I still always thought of myself as a photographer – I just wasn't in combat.

The future worked out well for us, although we lost an infant son, but our other two children are well, along with our three grandchildren, and Carol is still with me. I am truly blessed.

Carol and I had a wedding photography business from 1969 till the year 2000 when we retired. We've had a beekeeping business since 1980, and now in retirement we keep bees and sell honey.

I am proud of my service in Vietnam. Years ago, when our daughter was young, I remember looking at a world globe with her. I spun it around, found Vietnam, and I asked a question that still goes unanswered: "What the Hell were we doing there?"

64   *Cameras, Combat and Courage*

Tom Wong
Then
U.S. Army
Combat Photographer
69th Signal Battalion
HQ & HQ Company
Photo Platoon
Saigon
Republic of Vietnam

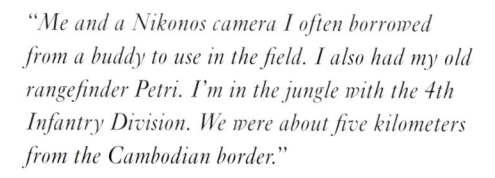

"Me and a Nikonos camera I often borrowed from a buddy to use in the field. I also had my old rangefinder Petri. I'm in the jungle with the 4th Infantry Division. We were about five kilometers from the Cambodian border."

Now
Retired
Port Orchard, Washington

What Doesn't Kill You Makes You Stronger

Tom Wong

I was a little surprised to get my "greeting" from Uncle Sam, but I shouldn't have been. I was twenty, the draft was in full swing, and I hadn't gone directly from high school to college. Enrolling in college was a way to avoid being drafted, so I knew my number would be coming up. I didn't want to be drafted so I went to the recruiter's office to find out about any options I might have. I could join for four years and choose my duty station, or three years and choose what training I wanted. Since I had taken a lot of German classes in high school, I really wanted to go to Germany. My high school buddy Mike Worley and I decided we would join at the same time and ask for Germany.

I recently had become interested in photography and the more I thought about it, the more it sounded like a good idea to pursue it further. Mike went with the Germany option, and ended up in the military police. After less than a year in Germany, he was sent to Vietnam. Ultimately, I decided I wanted to go to photography school, and enlisted for the three mandatory years.

On August 1, 1966, I boarded a military bus at the Seattle Induction Center, and headed off to Fort Lewis, Washington for Basic training.

Basic was the usual marching, physical training, etc. Line up for everything, and no talking in the mess hall. We never got to leave the company area without being marched. If you needed to buy something from the PX (Post Exchange), you got enough guys together who also wanted to go, got marched over, and marched back. Weekend passes? Not a chance!

There wasn't enough time after Basic to take leave, so I headed straight to Fort Monmouth, New Jersey, for still photo school. We flew to Philadelphia and took a bus from there to Fort Dix to drop off some guys before arriving at Fort Monmouth. Riding across New Jersey it seemed like almost every house had some kind of junk in the front yard, and I remember thinking it didn't look much like "The Garden State" that all the license plates said it was.

Photo school was classroom study and lots of hands-on camera training. We took photos on base and sometimes went in to nearby Red Bank to shoot. At night there was a reading assignment and workbook, then repeat the next day. We learned how to take

"This smell was like daisies, or dirty feet, and unlike the other smell, this one persisted from Long Binh all the way into Saigon. I later learned that it was the smell of bamboo shoots cooking. They taste a whole lot better than they smell."

Top and above: Saigon street vendors' carts.

aerials, including verticals, without getting your toes in the shot. We went to Fort Dix to take "combat" photos of the guys going through infantry training. I don't know if I thought much about what I would be photographing after school, but the times being what they were, I'm sure that Vietnam often came up in our BS sessions.

I went to New York City almost every weekend. I am half Chinese, and one of my Chinese aunts lived about two blocks from Chinatown. She was also part owner of a Chinese restaurant in Jersey, so she would bring food home on Friday and Saturday nights, plus we would go to Chinatown to eat. During the day, I would wander around New York taking pictures.

I think photo school was around thirteen weeks long. Early in February, 1967, orders for our class came down. The first several duty assignments weren't for Vietnam, and I thought I just might luck out. That didn't happen, and the next bunch of names, mine included, were all going to Vietnam in the middle of March. I was slightly excited, just to be going somewhere new, but also apprehensive because of the war.

After photo school I went home on my first leave. Even though I had really enjoyed the photo training, I was ready for a change. The thirty days passed in a hurry.

First stop was Oakland, California. I don't remember much about it, just that there was a large building with row after row of bunks with little room in between. I think I spent one night there before getting on the bus for Travis Air Force Base. From there we would fly to Vietnam.

The flight to Vietnam took seventeen hours. We stopped in Japan for fuel and food, and they had two large covered areas set up with places to sit. Each had room for one planeload of GIs and they were both full, so we had to remain sitting on the plane.

Arriving at Bien Hoa and stepping off the plane actually felt like getting hit. The heat and humidity were awful. As we were getting off the plane, there was a bunch of "grunts" (infantrymen) walking by with their M-16s. They were soaked with sweat and covered with dirt. We watched them go by, grim-faced. Some of them glanced at us, but without any acknowledgement. Some of them had dirt on their teeth! I had seen that in Basic when guys breathed through their mouths in the dust, but this wasn't training. It was a sobering sight.

The first trip to the mess hall made things look a little brighter when I saw quart cartons of milk on the tables. It was an illusion, however, as the milk was reconstituted and tasted awful. The food wasn't far behind.

Then there were the smells! I saw numerous columns of black smoke and when we got to Long Binh I learned that the smoke was the result of burning shit from the latrines. On the bus ride from Long Binh to Saigon, a different odor predominated. This one was like daisies, or dirty feet, and unlike the other smell, this one persisted from Long Binh all the way to Saigon. I later learned that it was the smell of bamboo shoots cooking. They taste a whole lot better than they smell.

68   Cameras, Combat and Courage

Not far inside the main gate at Tan Son Nhut Air Force Base, we turned off the main road and onto Camp Gaylor, headquarters of the 69th Signal Battalion. I don't remember a lot about the first few days there except that the supply room had no jungle fatigues or boots. I later learned they were both available on the black market downtown. I eventually got some out in the field by trading film for them.

Film could literally open doors. Everyone wanted a camouflaged poncho liner, but no one knew where to get one. I liked to stop at press camps on the way back from assignments, and the one at Qui Nhon had one on every rack. I asked about getting one and was told they didn't have any more. I pulled out a few outdated packs of color Polaroid film and offered them to the sergeant. He took me outside and opened the door on a conex storage container that was packed to the ceiling with them.

My first assignment was to photograph artillery at a place called Camp Carroll, up near the DMZ (De-Militarized Zone). The "Rock Pile" was to the west, and Khe Sahn to the southwest. It was a Marine base camp with Army artillery. The Stars and Stripes referred to the artillery as being Marine, and some General took offense to that and wanted pictures to prove it was Army artillery.

Camp Carroll was pretty stark – lots of tents and lots of dirt. The artillery was the 175mm M107s and I tried to get a picture of a projectile exiting the barrel, but that proved to be almost impossible. I did manage to catch one, but it was almost out of the frame. The prints were done in Hawaii, and when they came back, I couldn't believe they had cropped the projectile out!

Duty in Saigon was not too bad. We had fairly decent "hootches" as we called the barracks with concrete floors, so at least we weren't living in the mud during the monsoon season. The tin roofs were hot, but nowhere near as hot as a tent. When we were in the field, we always took a lot of heat about having hot showers in Saigon. The

Twin 40mm Duster gunner thought he saw something moving. I managed a lucky shot, with no tripod. The M42 "Duster" was a self-propelled anti-aircraft gun – each 40mm cannon could fire 120 rounds a minute. This was my first assignment, at Camp Carroll, up near the DMZ (De-Militarized Zone).

These photos were from various publicity assignments I had around Saigon. *Left:* California Congressman Craig Hosmer with a member of a local defense force. *Right:* General Westmoreland during a ceremony presenting M-16 rifles to the South Vietnamese Army. (My guess was that most of them would go unfired.)

only hot showers I had were when I wasn't in Saigon. Aircraft wing tanks, painted OD (olive drab) or black, and sitting in the sun all day made for fine, warm showers.

Probably the best part of being in Saigon was having a day off every week. That usually meant going to our photo supply room to get a few rolls of film, and then going to town to take photos. One of my buddies was a lab man, and I would give him my film when I got back to the hootch. He worked the graveyard shift and the next day I would have slides ready to cut up and be put in cardboard mounts.

Photo assignments in Saigon were the usual; awards, promotions etc., and worst of all, the passport section. It was a small room across the street from the photo section, away from all the guys, and you just had to be there if someone needed a passport photo. There was the ceremony with Gen. Westmoreland presenting the South Vietnamese Army with M-16s. I also photographed a group of congressmen as they toured several hamlets to see how some particular program was working. Once, a twin-engine plane lost its landing gear on takeoff at Tan Son Nhut, and I shot it landing, without incident, on a runway that had been foamed.

I traveled around the country quite a bit, especially while running down about fifteen commanding officers to take their portraits. I got to fly around in helicopters a lot, which I loved. While out with the Korean Tiger Division, I got to see just how effective hand grenades are when used for fishing in a river.

70   *Cameras, Combat and Courage*

Operation Hong Kil Dong was the largest South Korean operation of the war. Over 48 days, the Tiger and White Horse Divisions claimed a kill ratio of 24:1, or 638 enemy killed while only losing 26 of their own men. These are some of my photos from that operation. Clockwise from top left: Just off the choppers, Korean troops begin patrols. Another patrol up a muddy creek. Koreans with a suspected VC prisoner. He had a bloody nose – must have fallen. Troops crossing a river.

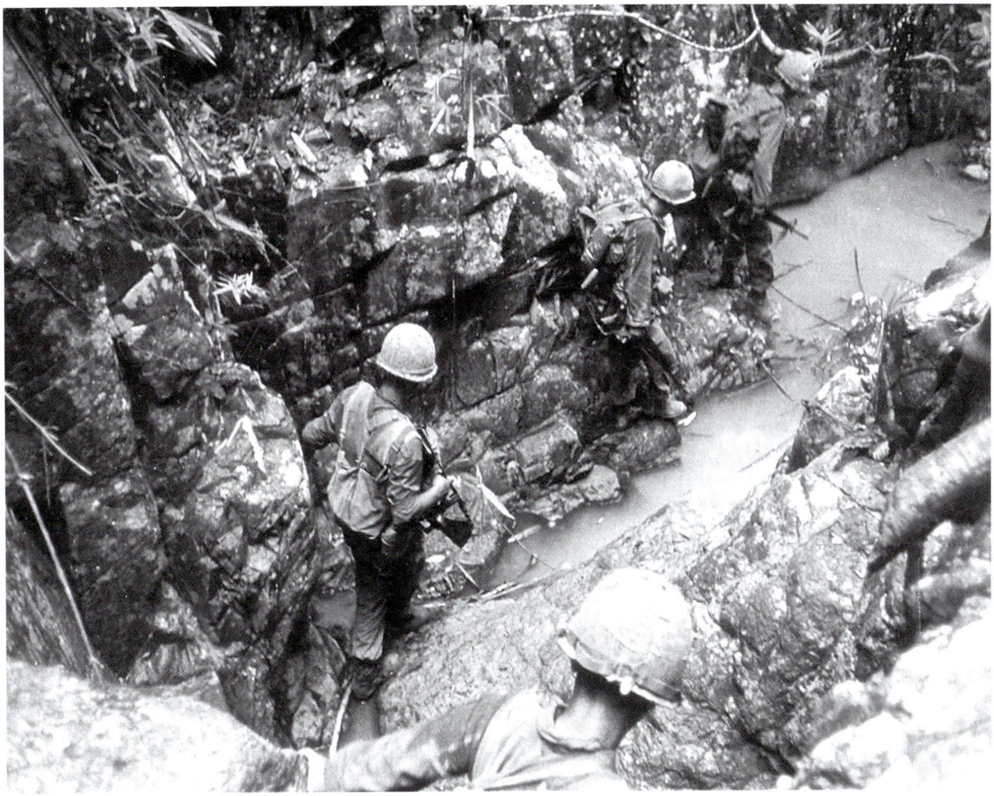

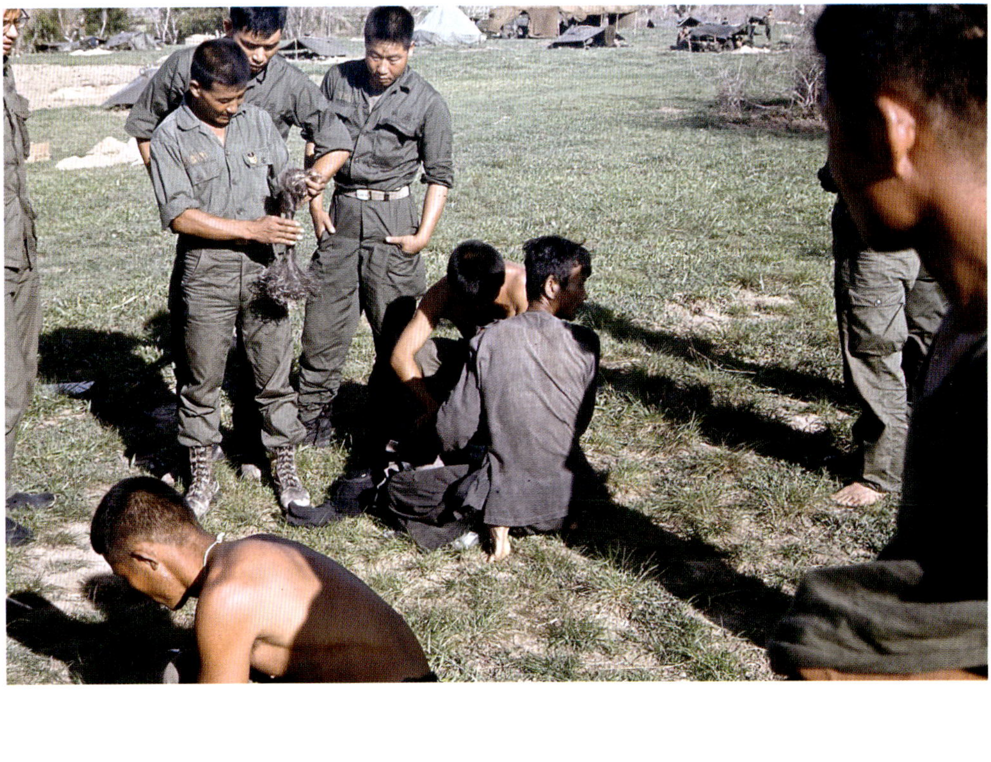

Camera gear consisted of a 4x5 Super Speed Graphic and a 35mm Pentax Spotmatic. I used the 4x5 for the commanders' portraits, even though lugging around the large case with a bunch of film holders was a pain. I also seem to remember dragging along a changing bag to unload and reload the film holders. I used to borrow a buddy's Nikonos underwater camera to take to the field. Nothing was automatic, and focus was done by looking at the subject, guessing the distance, and then turning the focus knob to that distance.

Another still photographer, Curt Parsons, and I were sent to the 9th Division at Bear Cat to photograph some part of Operation *Junction City*, I think, or maybe Operation *Cedar Falls*. We were to meet a lieutenant and accompany him to a different location. We waited a couple of days and he still hadn't shown up.

During that time, we talked with some 9th Infantry Division guys whose tents were nearby, and on the morning of the third day they told us they were going out on patrol. I told Curt we should go along. He disagreed. I kept trying to talk him into going, but he kept saying he thought the lieutenant was coming and wouldn't change his mind. Curt wasn't the type of guy who was afraid to do something, so I was a little surprised he was so against going on the patrol. It turned that the "LT" did show up later that morning, but before he did, we found out that five of the six guys on that patrol had been shot. I don't remember if we were told whether they were killed or wounded, but I do remember thinking it was a good patrol to have missed.

On another assignment we went out with a couple of companies of the 4th Infantry Division that were operating about five kilometers from Cambodia. We arrived at their base camp, a place called Jackson Hole, and checked in with S-2 (Intelligence). As usual, we got a briefing, and this time we were shown a map indicating there were several NVA (North Vietnamese Army) infantry units, divisions if I remember correctly, just over the border from the two companies we would be photographing. After our briefing, we asked about getting a "slick" (helicopter) out to where we were going. We were told it was too late; the last one for the day had just left.

We spent the night in camp and got a "Huey" (UH-1 helicopter) out early the next morning. When we arrived we found out they had taken small arms and mortar fire the night before, so everyone was busy with sand bags getting ready for more of the same. Finally some action, I thought, but how am I going to take photos in the dark?

A few hours before dark, a couple of F-4s (Phantom jets) bombed suspected enemy positions on the next ridge. They dropped large bombs and anti-personnel bombs that made the hillside sparkle like Christmas lights. It was quite a show, and we all stood around watching, hoping "Charlie" (the Viet Cong) was feeling the effects. I took a few shots, but didn't have a telephoto lens. It was a quiet night on our hill.

The next morning several squads headed out on patrol toward Cambodia, and we went with one of them. A couple of the guys found a small cache of ammo and Chinese hand grenades at the base of a tree, rigged it up, and detonated it. We continued on for a couple of hours, then turned around and headed back.

We came to a large area that had been bombed by B-52s. There's not much left when they're done. Some of the guys wanted take a bath in one of the bomb craters, so the squad leader put me and a couple of others on the perimeter.

It wasn't long before I thought I heard voices and movement coming from behind us. I told the squad leader, and he said another guy had heard it also. By the time everyone got their clothes back on, there was no doubt someone was coming behind us and all I could think about were those NVA division symbols on the map, and that our little squad could very well soon have a problem. Having a .45 pistol with only one clip, plus a couple of hand grenades seemed inadequate.

We started climbing up the hill to our camp. It was steep, and part way my legs were cramping up, probably because I hadn't taken my salt tablets. By the time we got to the top, I was beat and it didn't really register when one of the grunts said, "Watch out for the trip wire." Between "trip" and "wire" I hit and broke the wire. It went to a flare on the perimeter, and when they were hooking it back up, they set it off, setting the jungle on fire. The perimeter had been cleared some, so it wasn't a big fire and they put it out fairly quickly, but not before it had set a claymore mine on fire. I felt so special ...

The good news was it turned out the noises we heard behind us were from another one of our own patrols returning to camp. It was an uneventful trip. About two weeks

Life in the field. *Above left:* "Keep your finger off the trigger when cleaning your .45" was something I forgot as I sat in my deluxe accommodation in the back of a three-quarter ton truck. I was with the 9th Infantry near Bear Cat. *Above right:* Clearing a spot for my shelter half in the field with the 4th Infantry, about five clicks from the Cambodian border.

after leaving, those same companies were featured in the Stars and Stripes military publication. They had taken a real beating at Dak To.

To break the monotony, GIs would pull pranks on each other, and one day in particular, it was my turn to be on the receiving end. I was in the caption room, writing captions for my last assignment. It takes some concentration to be sure the names and units are correct, and that they are on the right photo. A couple of guys came in and sat a grenade down on the table right in front of me. It was painted orange, and I asked them where they had gotten it. They said it belonged to Wold, and he had painted it so no one would think it was real. I knew Wold had some real ones in his footlocker because he had added a couple I had when I returned from the field one time. I continued with my captions and the guys left after a short time. Several minutes later, Smitty came in and said, "Hey, there's a grenade." He pulled the pin and let the handle fall on the table. I backhanded it across the room, vaulted the table and ran out the door, and was greeted by several guys laughing their butts off.

Every day there was a duty roster posted for what was called "task force." We would go to the arms room and get a weapon, then load a "deuce and a half" (two and a half-ton truck) with ammo. We were restricted to the company area, and slept in our fatigues. If they blew the horn on the truck, we would load up and head out. They would run us out on Tan Son Nhut somewhere, and we would sit around out there for an uneventful hour or so, then head back to Camp Gaylor.

But in 1968, the first night of the Tet (Vietnamese New Year) offensive was a different story.

John Nielsen was a good friend. We had gone to the field together, since he was a motion picture guy, and he had task force duty that night. He had chosen to check the M-60 machine gun out of the arms room, since you didn't have to clean it when you turned it back in.

John's bunk was just inside the door to our hootch, and when I came back from the shower I hit my shin on the end of the barrel. I gave John a good-natured blast over it, and went on about my business. I never saw him again.

Early the next morning, I saw a couple of guys coming up the company street, ashen and bloody. They told me it was John's blood, and he had been killed. A while later, I saw his helmet in the orderly room, lying there with a bullet hole in it. The entrance hole was in the back. I kept reminding myself that when we were in the field, he would wear his helmet backward while filming.

John's death was pretty emotional for me. I was in disbelief and sad, and then surprised to feel intense anger. I have been angry many times, but this felt different. I wanted to kill someone, and I was shocked by the intensity of my feelings. As the morning wore on, there were reports that the VC were headed our way, using women and children as shields. Now, instead of wanting to kill, I was wondering if I would have

Some of the bomb damage from B-52 strikes. This is the area where I (on the right) tripped and broke a wire going to one of our perimeter flares. When they were hooking the wire back up, the flare went off and set the jungle on fire. It was quickly doused, but not before it set off a claymore anti-personnel mine. I felt so special …

the nerve to shoot, and risk killing an innocent woman or child. I played it out in my mind for a while. "Do you think you can hit just the VC at 200 yards? 100? 50? If there are women and children, can you pull the trigger at all?" I never did get comfortable with the thought and, thankfully, I didn't have to make the choice. The VC didn't make it that far. To this day, thinking about that morning makes me uncomfortable.

I had task force the next night, and needless to say, I couldn't sleep at all. Lying there dressed, including steel pot and flack jacket, I kept thinking that if they blew the horn, it wasn't going to be like playing "cops and robbers" in the front yard.

We had nightly guard duty for some time after the first night of Tet. One night, five of us were out by one end of the runway. There was a cement guard tower, and three guys decided to climb up in it. Another guy and I stayed down in the trench below.

After several hours, we heard a tank coming down the perimeter road toward us. It seemed like there was at least one flare in the sky most of the time, so we could also see the tank. Right near where we were, the road took a sharp left, but instead of turning, the tank stopped. We could hear the turret turning, and the next thing we knew, the barrel was pointed right at our position.

I heard someone on the tank say something about firing a round.

76   *Cameras, Combat and Courage*

John Nielsen was a good friend. *Above:* John lets a young Vietnamese girl peer through his Eyemo motion picture camera. *Below:* John with Vietnamese orphans during Christmas dinner. He was killed during the initial '68 Tet offensive on Tan Son Nhut air base, where our headquarters was located. His death was pretty emotional for me.

What Doesn't Kill You Makes You Stronger 77

I took this shot of the guard post at the Phu Tho Racetrack in Cholon during the 1968 Tet offensive. Cholon was a mostly Chinese part of Saigon.

More of the Cholon bombing damage. I was drawn to the child's cradle, now filled with cinder blocks and bricks.

Tet Offensive, 1968. I photographed what I remember as being the chapel at Tan Son Nhut Air Base just after it was hit by a rocket. Tan Son Nhut was also home to Camp Gaylor, our headquarters for the 69th Signal Battalion.

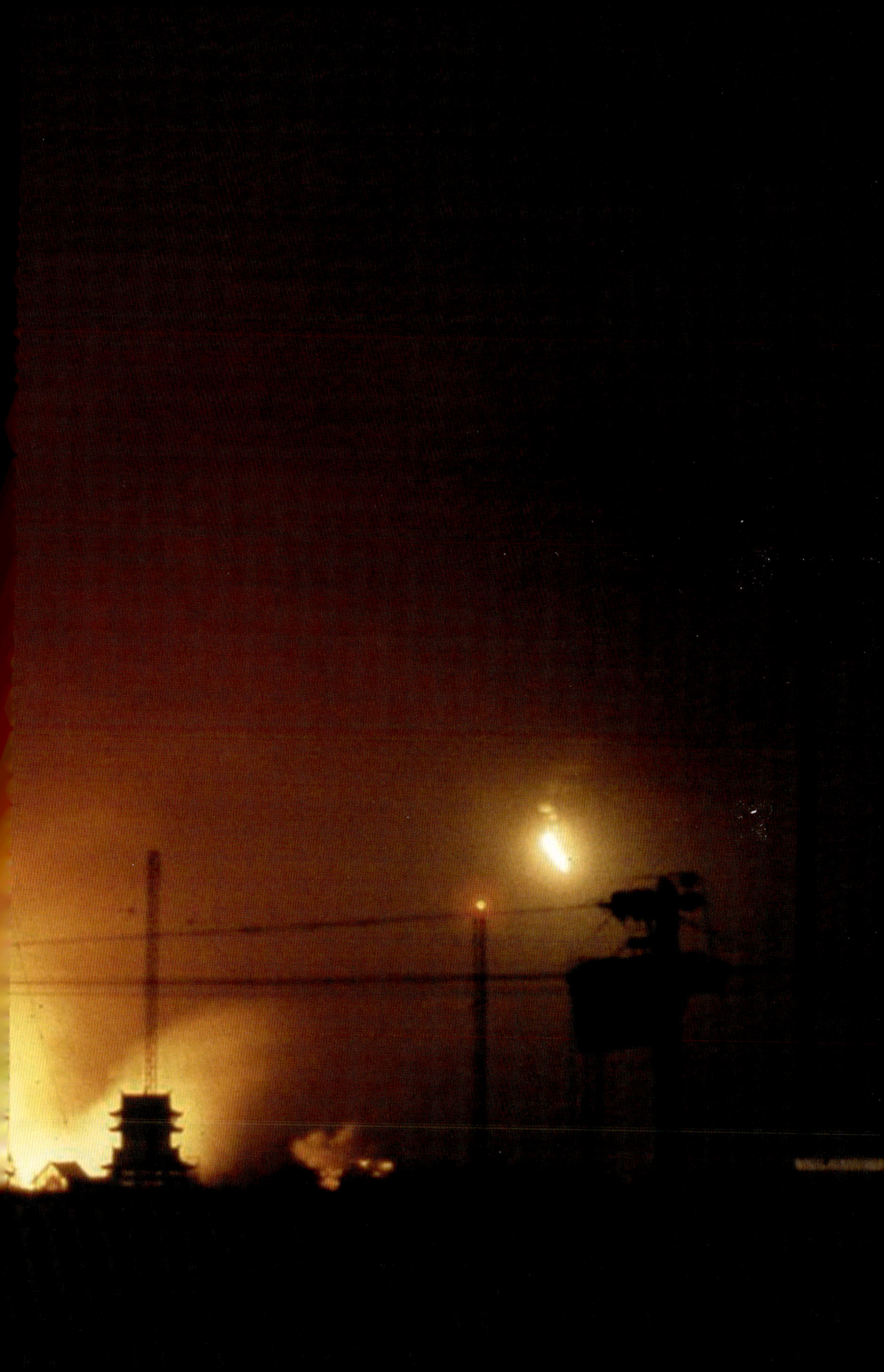

80   *Cameras, Combat and Courage*

Above: I took this wider view to show how extensive the destruction had been in Cholon. *Below:* This shot-up car was just in front of the U.S. Embassy. *Right:* I caught the rising smoke as the bombing of Cholon continued.

What Doesn't Kill You Makes You Stronger   81

82 *Cameras, Combat and Courage*

A soldier guards a bombed-out building in Cholon while Signal Corps guys were stringing wire to re-establish communications a day or so after the initial Tet attacks.

What Doesn't Kill You Makes You Stronger 83

More Cholon destruction.

84   *Cameras, Combat and Courage*

John Nielsen grabbed a shot of me out with the South Korean Tiger Division.

I whipped out my Zippo, lit it, and waved it in the air. I ran over to the tank and talked to them. They said they knew someone was there, but didn't know whom, and were going to fire a round.

Thank you, Zippo!

I didn't want to count down the number of days I had left in-country because it seemed like that would make the time go slower. The big Tet offensive took care of that, as I had about 45 days left, and the usual routine went out the window. Guard duty at night, KP, and for a couple of weeks there was the daily round or two of mortar or rocket fire somewhere on Tan Son Nhut.

As the days wore down, we did a lot of guessing and speculating about where our next duty station would be, and the thought of going home was on everyone's mind, and for me, a lot of curiosity about what the next chapter in my life would be.

After Vietnam, I was sent to Bamberg, Germany. Still photographers weren't authorized on the entire post, but the Army sent three of us. Because I could speak German, I was assigned to the Public Affairs Office, where I did some translating of newspaper articles and took photos of all of the German-American events. The other two guys were reassigned to Stuttgart.

My fiancée came over from the States, and we got married. I got to spend sixteen months in the country – longer than my buddy who had signed up for Germany.

After being discharged, I got a two-year degree in commercial photography, and took photos for the Department of Defense at a Navy Yard, and for the Army Corps of Engineers. I eventually ended up on the process camera at a Navy printing office. Not exactly photography, but a lot of the fundamentals I learned in photo school were a definite plus. I retired from the printing office several years ago.

Even with all the usual things there are to complain about in the Army, overall I would have to say it was a positive experience in my life, including Vietnam. A lot of guys grow up while in the military, and I think that was true for me too. I learned I could do more than I thought I could, and put up with more than I thought I could. In other words, I learned something about myself. Thanks to my mother's prayers, I didn't have to witness the truly ugly, brutal side of war, nor did I die there.

"What doesn't kill you makes you stronger," as the saying goes.

Christopher Jensen

Then
U.S. Army
Combat Motion Picture Photographer
221st Signal Company
Long Binh
Republic of Vietnam

Now
"*I live in The White Mountains of New Hampshire and do freelance reporting for The New York Times, New Hampshire Public Radio and The New Hampshire Center for Public Interest Journalism.*"

"Here I am out on a mission. My 16mm Filmo is just under my left arm. I also carried a pair of Nikons for my personal photography."

From Phnom Penh to Ripcord:
The Free Range Motion Picture Photographer

Christopher Jensen

In 1968, I was a photojournalism major at Ohio State University. I was doing fine in photojournalism and freelancing for Associated Press but neglecting all my other courses. One day, as an alternative to studying harder, I decided a reasonable option was to enlist in the Army.

I figured everybody was supposed to go into the Army. So, I would get it out of the way and return to college.

A helpful recruiter suggested I enlist as a medic, so I signed the papers and headed back to meet some college friends. At that point a girl nicely told me that all the medics

SEAPC (Southeast Asia Pictorial Center) / 221st Signal Company at Long Binh. The photo lab is on the left, operations is in the center, and audio-visual processing is the building on the right. (*Photo courtesy of 221st Commanding Officer Capt. William Ruth's Unit History e-book*)

get killed. I admitted that point had escaped me and getting killed seemed – at first glance – to be problematic.

The next day I switched to photography in exchange for a three-year commitment instead of the usual two years that draftees got. On November 22, 1968 I was sworn in.

At Fort Monmouth, New Jersey, I trained as a motion picture guy, an 84C MOS (Military Occupational Specialty) designation. Our class graduated and almost everyone went to Vietnam. But one other guy and I were sent to Fort Hood, Texas. The speculation was that an armored division was probably gearing up for Vietnam and we would be assigned to it. That assumed that the United States Army operated in a logical way, which I was to learn was not always true.

We showed up at Personnel in Fort Hood and were told that nobody cared what we were trained to do. Fort Hood needed armored reconnaissance scouts. I was assigned to an armored unit and it seemed that as "armor-less" scouts we were supposed to sneak around and with our dying breaths radio American tanks the location of the Soviet tanks. A noble sacrifice to be sure.

Happily I wrangled a transfer to the post newspaper and worked there as a reporter and photographer. But Fort Hood was hot and miserable and boring and I decided to volunteer for Vietnam. I was waiting until Friday the 13th to send through my request. But the Army – personnel office scamps that they were – beat me to it. I got orders to report to Vietnam in April 1970.

I was assigned to the 221st Signal Company in Long Binh and was initially suspected of being a narc. But then I ran into guys from my mopic (motion picture) class, eliminating that suspicion.

I would spend 15 months with the 221st Signal. At the end of my 12 months I agreed to spend an extra three months in-country, which was part of the Army's "early-out" program. If – upon your return to the United States – you had six months or less, the Army would let you call it quits. I liked the idea of Vietnam a lot better than going back to someplace like Ft. Hood.

We had an amazing amount of freedom, going where we wanted to go without anyone telling us to shoot happy pictures. We were supposed to do straight documentary photography.

During those 15 months our team covered operations ranging from the swamp known as the U Minh Forest in the Delta to the mountains around the A Shau Valley in I Corps. We went with Americans as well as ARVNs (Army of the Republic of Vietnam – the South Vietnamese Army).

Basically we did what everyone else in the unit we were covering did. We sat on top of APCs (Armored Personnel Carriers) churning along, inhaling the dust and diesel fumes and waiting for something to happen. And we humped through the mountains of I Corps, the swamps of the Delta, and the flatter lands of III Corps.

We picked land leeches off from the tops of our jungle boots and ate C-rations and were quickly recalibrated to a new lifestyle. Once, without a second thought, I joined ARVNs in filling my canteens from a huge earthen jar at the bottom of which sat what appeared to be a huge, happy lizard. I imagine he did not leave that jar when nature called.

Getting good motion pictures while moving through the jungle was tricky. It could be dark. Usually the vegetation blocked a reasonable view. If I paused a while to get the guys moving past I'd have to work harder to catch up. Not picture perfect.

And at the end of the day, the company or troop would settle into a night-defensive position. I'd blow up my air mattress (always good for a witty quip from somebody about "You're hired") and then make a little circle around it with insect repellent, an effort to keep crawling things away.

My two constant companions in the field – the 16mm Filmo and the M-79 "thumper." (*Photo by Sp.4 James Saller, 221st Signal Company*)

I carried my Filmo camera with 10 rolls of 16mm film, each 100 feet long. The Filmo was a heavy motion picture camera that operated by a spring. Winding the key-type knob would run film for about three minutes. It had a turret with normal, telephoto and wide-angle lenses. There was no autofocus and no light meter. We guessed at the lighting and tried to remember to set the distance. It usually worked out okay.

I carried two Nikons for my personal use. They hung around my neck. My Filmo was over the shoulder but so convenient I could walk with my hand on it.

I'm guessing I carried about 60 pounds of crap, including camera gear, C-rations, lots of water, a thin blanket called a poncho liner, an air mattress and a few personal items, like a spare set of socks, toothbrush and insect repellent.

Our standard weapon was a .45. But I quickly got tired of grunts making snide remarks about "dinky pistols." I imagined I would be more welcome with a real weapon.

Some other photographers continued with the .45s, taking the logical position that if things really went wrong they could use an M-16 or something that a wounded or dead American didn't need. But I thought it would be nice to have a more meaningful weapon to help out, particularly at night when there wasn't any photography, should things get really bad.

"Prior to crossing this river in the U Minh Forest, I stopped to photograph the ARVN troops as they reached the other side. The sawed-off butt of my M-79 grenade launcher is hanging from the right side of my rucksack. U Minh was more like one big swamp than a forest."

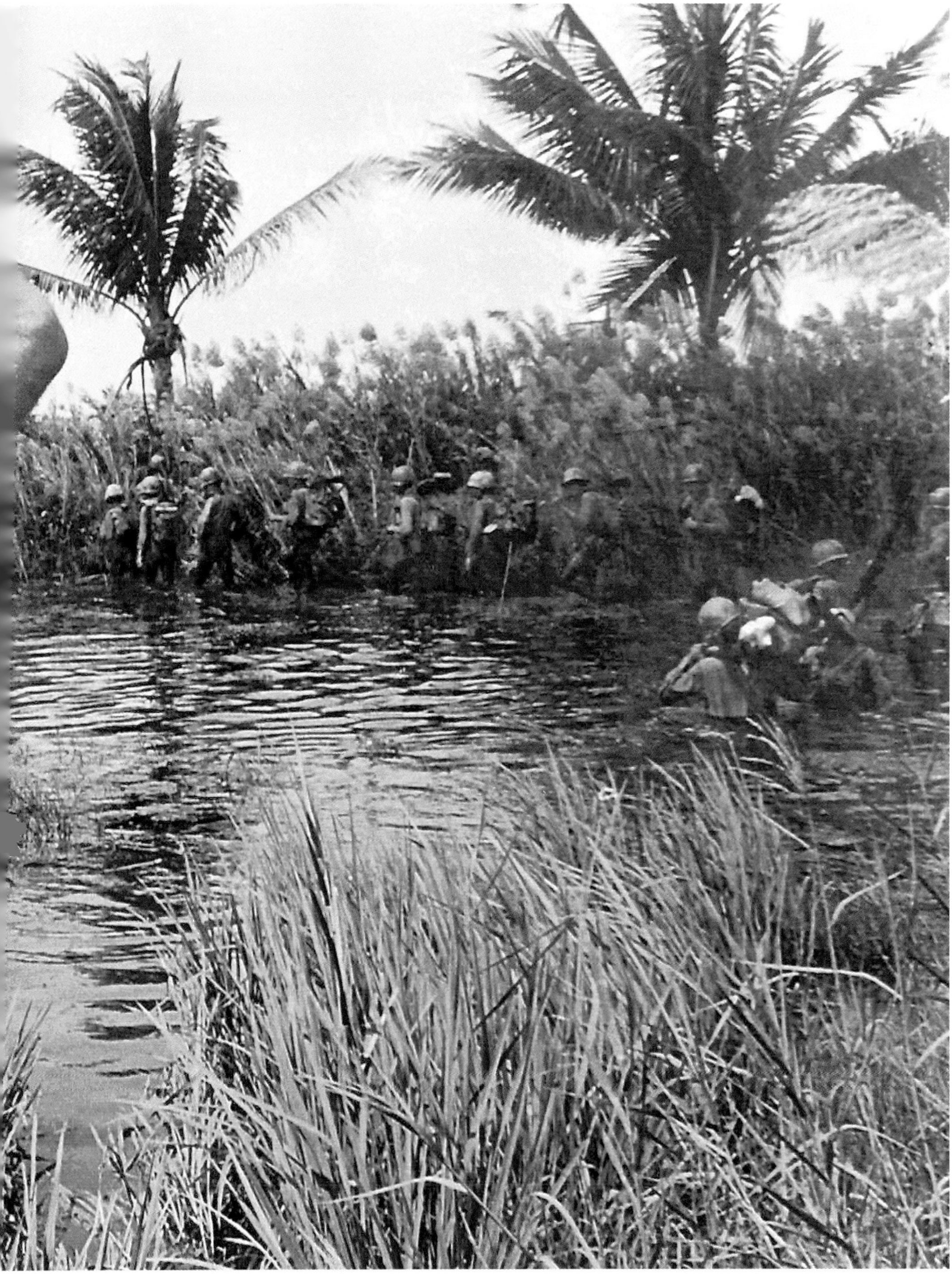

92   *Cameras, Combat and Courage*

The U Minh Forest, 1970: Often we spent time with Vietnamese soldiers ranging from the mountains of I Corps to the most southern part of the Delta. This included the U Minh Forest.

The U Minh Forest was a huge, swampy area and it was alluring because of the story that 500 French paratroopers dropped into it in 1952 and never emerged.

So, we waded and slogged along with the ARVNs. I spoke French with the officer. The American advisor, hurt somehow, left on the slick that brought us in. Surprise.

From Phnom Penh to Ripcord 93

Frames from film footage taken by Sp.4 Christopher Jensen, 221st Signal Company.

I didn't want an M-16 because it was too long and bulky. Another photographer bought me a .45 Thompson M1A1 submachine gun on the black market. The big wooden stock could be unscrewed and it came with a nice sling.

So, I tried that for a month or so. I looked darned picturesque but it was heavy and not thought to be very accurate at any distance. A group of ARVNs once gestured to me that it sucked as a weapon. Apparently they were not familiar with the panache of *The Untouchables*.

The Thompson also required .45 caliber ammunition and nobody else carried that. So, once I was out of ammo, the Thompson would just be a stylish and worthless accessory. I sold it to a guy with an armored unit, because he could carry lots and lots of .45 ammo on his APC.

I finally settled on a grenade launcher called an M-79, also known as a "thumper." It also came from the black market. I cut down the stock and the barrel, making it into a kind of pistol. It ruined the long-distance accuracy but this continued my olive-drab theme of being an inept soldier.

I carried the thumper attached to my rucksack and had not only high-explosive 40 mm rounds (Think: "little hand grenades") but also rounds that were like big shotgun shells. Designed for close-in they would send double-aught buckshot shrieking as they went out into the jungle.

In 15 months I fired at people twice. Once was with the Thompson during a sapper attack at night. The other was with the M-79 during Operation *Dewey Canyon II* near Khe Sanh. It is a good thing the war effort did not depend exclusively on my expertise as a soldier.

Normally we'd be gone a week or so until we ran out of film. Then we'd jump onto a resupply helicopter and hitch rides on C-130s back to Long Binh. We'd get cleaned up, write captions for our film, goof off a few days and go back out.

Cambodia

My first time in the bush was for the Cambodian invasion.

The officers divided us into groups sending us out with different units. I didn't understand how these decisions were made, but they turned out to involve life-and-death.

One group went to Pleiku and all five died when their helicopter – Ghostrider 079 – crashed. It was never clear if the Huey was shot down or suffered a mechanical failure.

I went with a lieutenant and was told there might be some American POWs to be rescued. We were to join Al Rockoff, a legendary veteran still photographer who was already in the bush.

The "real" Rockoff with us in Vietnam. (*Photo courtesy of 221st Commanding Officer Capt. William Ruth's Unit History e-book*)

John Malkovich portrayed the "movie" Rockoff in *The Killing Fields*. Rockoff went back to Cambodia as a civilian photographer and in 1975 found himself on the wrong end of a Khmer Rouge pistol. (Yes, he lived to tell about it.) Rockoff hated how he was portrayed in the film. It's a long story; see the movie for all the details.

We were with the 11th ACR (Armored Cavalry Regiment) and for days we rode through Cambodia perched on top of APCs. I filmed the column of APCs and tanks moving through the countryside and guys with minesweepers walking ahead of the tanks in a rubber plantation.

One day we stopped and watched a B-52 strike. Then we moved in to what had been an NVA (North Vietnamese Army) base camp. Huge craters. A few pith helmets. Lots of captured supplies. I filmed that, too.

I loved it. I was 21 years old and filthy dirty, but covering a major operation. It was the most exciting thing I'd ever done.

Cambodia and Richard Nixon's Silly Rule

I blame Rockoff.

We were in Long Binh when Al had this somewhat bold idea. There were reports that the Cambodians were killing ethnic Vietnamese. That seemed pretty likely, since there were news reports of lots of bodies floating down the Mekong River.

Rockoff said he heard there were concentration camps in Phnom Penh (Cambodia) and maybe we should go there.

Here was the problem: Rockoff and President Nixon were in conflict.

President Nixon promised there would be no American troops beyond something like 19 miles into Cambodia and Phnom Penh was way beyond that.

But Rockoff figured we should give it a try, following the philosophy of: What are they going to do to us? Send us to Vietnam?

Plus, Rockoff was a highly admired combat photographer and Richard Nixon was just the President of the United States.

Clearing mines during the Cambodian Invasion, 1970: My first time in the bush was with a cavalry troop going into Cambodia. During the days we sat on top of APCs or tanks and filmed as we churned along.

We spent one night in a rubber plantation. There was only one road out and there was a justifiable concern that it might have been mined during the night.

So, a team swept the road as we photographed. The hope was the only mines would need the weight of a tank to set them off. We didn't find any.

From Phnom Penh to Ripcord 97

Frames from film footage taken by Sp.4 Christopher Jensen, 221st Signal Company.

98   Cameras, Combat and Courage

Nixon finally admitted he was sending troops into Cambodia on April 11, 1970. Here he is pointing out NVA sanctuaries along the Cambodian border during his speech to the American people announcing the "Cambodian Incursion." (Or maybe he was saying "What the hell are Jensen and Rockoff doing in Phnom Penh???")

This is a "press pass" issued to me by the Cambodian government. It says that Christopher Jensen is "authorized to undertake the risks and perils in the regions of …" Then the hand writing lists the various provinces. It was alright with them for me and Rockoff to be there, but unfortunately our military superiors didn't agree.

We never told anyone what we were doing. We just said we were headed back to Cambodia and off we went. Nobody really asked for any details. Things were that flexible at the 221st as long as they thought you weren't goofing off and you wanted to go to the bush. Not everyone did.

We hitched a ride on a patrol boat up the Mekong River to Neak Luong, right at the border. We spent the night with some American advisors and took a ferry across the river. A carton of cigarettes got us a civilian taxi ride to Phnom Penh.

At one point, a guy in black pajamas with an AK-47 came out of the jungle to stop the vehicle and that seemed, arguably, to be a bad sign. I apparently worried Rockoff by pulling out my .45 pistol (that I was still carrying) with the idea I could shoot him through the car door. But the guy was with some Cambodian militia.

We got a hotel room in Phnom Penh and did photograph some compounds in which ethnic Vietnamese were being held. Not quite concentration camps, but not nice either.

It was very odd. We were strolling around in our jungle fatigues wondering if some civilian journalist might notice that we were oddly dressed for civilians and conclude that we were, well, somewhat beyond the line Richard Nixon had drawn in the jungle. Maybe we'd make the cover of *Life*.

It wasn't a reporter, but the military attaché from the U.S. Embassy who found us. We were at a sidewalk café having a beer one afternoon when this vehicle with U.S. flags pulled up. Out came a guy who wondered just who we were and what were we doing? He utterly failed to appreciate our initiative and sternly ordered us out of town. So we went back to the hotel, got our stuff, and went home the same way we got there.

Having gone to Phnom Penh and back was a head-shaking surprise to our bosses at Long Binh who were stunned at our combination of audacity, stupidity and luck, with the emphasis on the last two.

Fire Support Base Ripcord

Early in July, we heard there was a lot of trouble at a fire support base called Ripcord in I Corps near the Laotian border. Jim Saller and another mopic guy, Jerry Dubro, and I headed north.

The usual routine for going out with a unit was to stop at the Public Information Office (PIO) for the division and let them know. Then they would point us in the general direction of a helicopter likely to be carrying supplies out to a unit – or to a string of helicopters getting ready for a combat assault.

In this case we went to the 101st Airborne Division PIO at Camp Eagle. But the PIO there told us that no photographers, military or civilian, were allowed. This was odd, we thought, and interesting.

I'm shooting the action at Fire Support Base (FSB) Ripcord. Jim Saller, Jerry Dubro and I were the only photographers – military or civilian – to reach the besieged base. The battle, already three months old, went on for 23 more days and would turn out to be the last major ground battle between U.S. ground forces and the North Vietnamese Army. (*Photo by Sp.4 James Saller, 221st Signal Company*)

We decided to try anyway and went to the dust-off pad, where the medevac (medical evacuation) helicopters would lift off. We asked a couple of pilots if the next time a dust-off headed for Ripcord might we please, go along? They agreed.

A few hours later we were jumping out of a "slick" (UH-1 helicopter, or "Huey") at Ripcord. We were confronted by the commander, Lt. Col. Andre Lucas, who wanted to know "Who were we?"

I explained and asked if we could get out with the grunts in the bush. Lucas said that was absolutely not going to happen, but we were welcome to stay at the fire support base. He had somebody get us helmets and flak jackets, which normally we did not carry because they were heavy and it is hard to wear a helmet and shoot film and we were stupid.

Lucas probably saved some – if not all – our lives by not allowing us to get out with the grunts in the mountains directly surrounding Ripcord where there was a real horror show going on.

All that happened there was later detailed in the amazing book by Keith Nolan, *Ripcord: Screaming Eagles Under Siege*. But the short version is that there was serious fighting with NVA determined to annihilate those companies, part of an effort to stop American interference with its nearby operations.

We would not have been the best guys to help. We were all trained as photographers but the Army never gave us any additional training in being a "grunt" – your basic infantryman. It was on-the-job stuff which is less than ideal.

The NVA were also clearly interested in forcing the U.S. off the fire support base at which incoming fire was a regular event. We spent our time photographing the operations at Ripcord: artillery crews firing into the jungle to support the grunts, helicopters coming and going.

One morning I was filming and Jim Saller was shooting stills a little higher up and behind me. Suddenly there was an explosion up there and warm, wet stuff landed all over the back of my neck. I was sure a mortar had landed next to Saller who had been, well, disassembled. Happily, Saller had moved, and the hot, wet stuff was Spanish Rice flown into the base as a hot meal and stored in a Mermite can. Good luck for Saller. Not so good for those who wanted hot chow.

Saller, however, was not going to escape Ripcord unwounded.

Another day we were talking next to the roof of a bunker dug into the ground where we had our stuff. I decided to get something from the bunker and jumped down into the trench that led to our door. I had just hit the ground when there was a small explosion and Saller yelled those classic words: "I'm hit."

My first, arguably selfish thought, was: Wow, good timing on my part.

Indeed, Saller had been peppered up the side with shrapnel. Not fun, but luckily he wasn't hit in the throat or someplace vital, and months later we were calling him "Scarbody."

He still needed to leave Ripcord, and we decided Dubro should go with him in case he needed help. I wanted to stay until I either ran out of film or somebody came back for me.

I stuck around a few more days, shooting film as the NVA upped the ante and began sending huge 120mm mortars into the base in addition to the 82mm mortars they had been using. These bigger ones were easily damaging bunkers that had survived the 82mm impacts. They also indicated a seriousness of purpose on the part of the NVA.

Eventually I was out of film and was less than thrilled with those intrusive 120 mm mortars. I decided to head back and jumped on a Huey. I was asked to take part of a 120 mm mortar and give it to somebody from the 101st Intelligence, which I did.

At Camp Eagle I ran into John Luckey and a crew from the 221st Signal. They had just arrived. But I dissuaded them from us going back to Ripcord. We weren't being allowed to go out with the grunts and we already had hundreds of feet of film of guys firing out-going and living with incoming. It didn't seem like there was much to gain, plus I was tired and dirty and did I mention those big-ass mortars?

That was a huge mistake or incredibly lucky. Multiple choice.

102   Cameras, Combat and Courage

Fire Support Base Ripcord, 101st Airborne, July, 1970: Since our request to go out with the grunts was refused by Lt. Col. Lucas our time on Ripcord was basically spent roaming the firebase, which was quite large and buffeted by high winds.

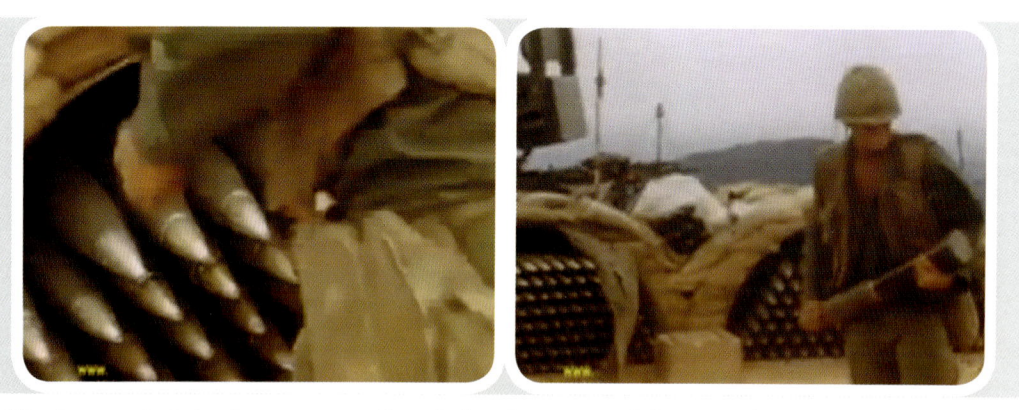

We photographed the almost constant fire missions in support of the grunts in the jungle around the base, as counter-mortar fire or in the case of one 105 mm exchanging fire with a .51 caliber machine gun manned by the NVA near the base of our hill.

We also photographed re-supply, medevacs and an arty guy who was startled by a mortar landing behind us and moved into the recoil of the 105 mm which didn't do any good for his leg.

From Phnom Penh to Ripcord 103

Frames from film footage taken by Sp.4 Christopher Jensen, 221st Signal Company

Me crossing a mountain stream in I Corps with ARVN troops. Moments earlier an ARVN soldier lost his footing and was swept downstream. Saller and I had been covering FSB O'Reilly in I Corps that the ARVNs decided to abandon since the NVA were starting to lay siege to it as they had done with the nearby FSB Ripcord. The entire base packed up and charged off one morning walking as quickly as possible through the mountains trying to reach a very distant extraction point before the NVA could react.

Days later, the siege of Ripcord intensified, as detailed in Keith Nolan's book. A Chinook helicopter was shot down onto the base, not far from the bunker where we stayed. It caught fire, a trapped crewman burned to death, and the flames set off lots of artillery rounds.

Life got very bad very quickly. Incoming increased and apparently the generals had no interest that late in the war in having a long, drawn-out fight that could wind up like another Khe Sanh.

So the base was abandoned under fire. Lt. Col. Lucas, who had allowed us to stay, was among those killed. He was awarded the Medal of Honor, a controversial move with some critics contending he'd done a poor job as a commander and the award was just a gift from the old-boy officer network.

Nolan's well-documented tally showed 74 Americans died on or around Ripcord, including 13 who were missing in action. There were 400 wounded.

Jim Saller took this photo of one of the 101st Airborne guys at Ripcord getting his evening chow from a "Mermite" can like the one that splattered Spanish Rice (and NOT Saller) all over me after a nearby explosion from an incoming mortar.

"One morning I was filming and Jim Saller was shooting stills a little higher up and behind me. Suddenly there was an explosion up there and warm, wet stuff landed all over the back of my neck. I was sure a mortar had landed next to Saller who had been, well, disassembled. Happily, Saller had moved, and the hot, wet stuff was Spanish Rice flown into the base as a hot meal and stored in a Mermite can. Good luck for Saller. Not so good for those who wanted hot chow."

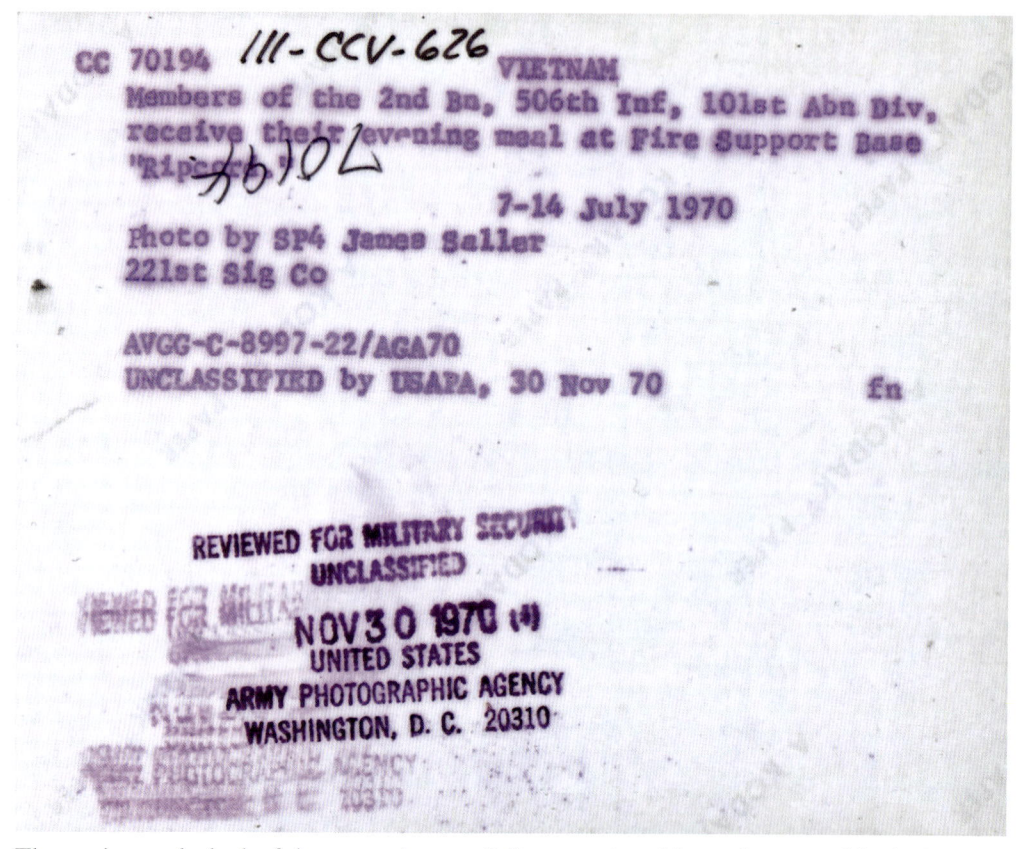

```
CC 70194  III-CCV-626  VIETNAM
Members of the 2nd Bn, 506th Inf, 101st Abn Div,
receive their evening meal at Fire Support Base
"Ripcord"
                            7-14 July 1970
Photo by SP4 James Saller
221st Sig Co

AVGG-C-8997-22/AGA70
UNCLASSIFIED by USAPA, 30 Nov 70                    fn

       REVIEWED FOR MILITARY SECURITY
              UNCLASSIFIED
              NOV 30 1970
              UNITED STATES
          ARMY PHOTOGRAPHIC AGENCY
          WASHINGTON, D. C. 20310
```

The caption on the back of that same photo, as Saller wrote it and it was later stored in the National Archives in Washington, D.C. That's where most of the photos by military photographers ended up, as well as the motion picture footage that I and others shot.

    Had we gone back, we could have filmed a hugely dramatic event. Of course some of us might have been killed, too.

    We still got the only professional film and mopic of Ripcord. But my recommendation meant we missed an amazing opportunity.

From Phnom Penh to Ripcord 107

I took these photos of the ruins of the Special Forces camp at Kham Duc that was overrun by the North Vietnamese in May of 1968. The top one shows bunkers in the foreground, just inside the wire. We wandered around, rummaging through the wreckage for souvenirs, oblivious to the potential danger from unexploded ordnance and booby traps. I found a rusted grease gun, but threw it away later.

Sapper Attack At Kham Duc

Normally we worked in three-man teams, but early in August we had a four-person team for reasons that now escape me. There was Jim Saller, John Luckey, Larry Brock and myself.

We went to Kham Duc, which was up north and close to the Laotian border. It was the site of a former Special Forces camp overrun in 1968. But in the summer of 1970 it was also the location of part of Operation *Elk Canyon I*, which was another effort to make life miserable for the NVA in the area, including those moving along the supply route known as the Ho Chi Minh Trail.

There was a battered runway complete with the wreckage of a C-130 from 1968.

And there were the ruins of the Special Forces camp.

One of the dumb things we did was to wander over to that camp and rummage around, taking photos of the wrecked bunkers and fighting positions. I even took a rusted grease gun as a souvenir, only to throw it away later. None of us were smart enough to think that there was a lot of unexploded ordnance around and the place might have been booby-trapped.

At the adjacent artillery compound there were 105 and 155 mms, and we were told to make ourselves at home in a partially dug position. Until a few days earlier it had been used by a quad-fifty machine gun but it had been moved elsewhere.

It didn't occur to us to object to being put in a position with nothing between us and the rolls and rolls of concertina wire. In retrospect, it is clear that we were seen as canaries in the Kham Duc coal mine, expendable because we weren't friends with anyone in the unit.

We took turns with guard duty. Two on and two off. In yet another demonstration of new-country dumbness, from time to time I would turn on a flashlight and check the wire. This, I figured, might deter anyone from trying to come through in our area. I knew it would also show somebody with a rocket-propelled grenade where we were but I thought it was worth it. It is possible I was not a tactical genius and I lacked self-preservation skills.

I don't remember with whom I had guard duty the night we were attacked. There were explosions and weapons firing with the North Vietnamese sappers (commandos) inside the base, which is not the ideal tactical situation.

I remember saying something dumb like "Don't shoot unless you have a target," which was wrong, I later learned. I was thinking about conserving ammunition. We should have been shooting the shit out of the whole area in front of us.

Then somebody from the 105mm battery behind us ran up and told us to duck – a courteous gesture, because they were going to fire a "fletchette" (also known as a "beehive") round over our heads. Unlike a high-explosive round, beehive rounds are

While at Kham Duc in 1970, I photographed the wreckage of this C-130 from the 1968 attack. It turned out to be the plane flown by Lt. Col. John Delmore. He took fire while attempting to land and crashed into a CH-47 Chinook helicopter that had been destroyed earlier in an effort to not block the runway. The five-man crew got out and were rescued by soldiers twenty minutes later. More planes continued the heroic evacuation attempts, culminating in the event described on the next page.

110   *Cameras, Combat and Courage*

This was taken during the 1968 attack and evacuation. It shows a C-123 on the runway (top center) as it awaits three members of an Air Force Combat Control Team (CCT) that had been reinserted (under protest from pilot Lt. Col. Jay Van Cleeff who was ordered to reinsert them) to coordinate the final evacuation, even though everyone was either dead or already evacuated. By then the North Vietnamese had taken the camp and as Van Cleeff took off, he heard another C-130 pilot saying the camp was empty and could now be destroyed. He quickly notified all aircraft in the area that he had just reinserted the CCT, and to not destroy the camp. Shortly thereafter, the C-123 piloted by Lt. Col. Joe M. Jackson landed under heavy fire to extract the team. They can be seen in the photo, running up the right side of the runway to Jackson's plane. He successfully flew them out to Da Nang. The next day, 60 B-52s bombed the camp.

For his heroism, Jackson was awarded the Medal of Honor.

The above photograph is the only one that ever recorded actions leading to the award of a Medal of Honor.

Lt. Col. Joe M. Jackson and the Air Force Medal of Honor.

GI checks out a makeshift "Bangalore Torpedo" left by the sappers. It's one or more connected tubes, usually metal, that holds an explosive charge and is used to blow up an obstacle, in this case the wire at the Kham Duc perimeter. This is a crude one fashioned from bamboo.

I caught John Luckey photographing the ruins of the Special Forces camp overrun in '68. Unexploded mortars and stuff? What could go wrong?

filled with nasty little metal darts designed to repel ground attacks. We got as far down as we could and at least one round went over our heads. I remember seeing a ripple of dust along the ground in front of us, out through the wire and into the jungle.

It seemed that it should be a once-in-a-lifetime experience, so we decided to quickly relocate and split up. It now reminds me of the "Run Away! Run Away!" routine involving the knights in *Monty Python and the Holy Grail.*

I took cover under a metal culvert with a few sandbags on top. I joined a guy with an M-60 machine-gun that was incredibly, painfully loud. I joined in, firing my Thompson.

At one point I remember seeing some GIs pause over several downed sappers and fire into them, apparently to make sure they were dead. Things were still in flux; it was no time to try taking prisoners and nobody was taking chances. I can't imagine they weren't already dead. But it was stunning.

By dawn it was over. We could see some of the sappers – brave young men – that had come through the wire to the right of our position where they blew up another bunker. I always wondered whether the flashlight – or just plain dumb luck – played a part in that.

Three Americans died in the attack, including a medic tending a wounded soldier. Some equipment was damaged. Sixteen sappers were killed, mostly inside the wire. One attention-getter was a Bangalore torpedo, still under the wire. That suggested the plan was to blow a hole so more NVA could get inside. But before the sapper could trigger the explosive he was killed.

Note: Early in 2013, I posted the film I took of the dead sappers on YouTube. That started an exchange with Vietnamese who said they recognized family members and wondered Where did we bury them?

I began working with a couple of guys from that artillery unit who were eager to help even though one had been wounded and the other lost a good friend in the attack. With maps and photos and memories, they tried to pinpoint a spot from 43 years earlier. In the summer of 2013, that effort was still underway.

One of the people with whom I was e-mailing said he was a rookie sapper with the battalion that sent the attackers at Kham Duc. He wasn't part of the attack, but knew the men who were. Of all things we are now Facebook friends.

Lam Son 719 / Dewey Canyon II

Early in 1971, the military decided it would be a swell idea to have the ARVNs go into Laos to disrupt North Vietnamese operations. The operation would be called *Lam Son 719*.

From Phnom Penh to Ripcord 113

At the Laotian border during Dewey Canyon II. Left to right, me, Tom Wolzien, and Jim Saller. Wolzien was a lieutenant and went out with us mainly to provide adult supervision.

Henri Huet (left) and Larry Burrows (right) before their fateful flight into Laos. The marker post between them is the exact spot where the three of us are standing in the photo above. You can see the same post just behind me on the left side of the picture. We had shared the spot with gods.

114   Cameras, Combat and Courage

The last shot of (left to right) Shimamoto, Huet, Burrows, and Potter, taken by U.S. Marine photographer Sergio Ortiz.

The Americans would provide support from Vietnam, primarily along Route Nine, using the abandoned Marine base at Khe Sanh. That part would be called *Dewey Canyon II*. This was a huge deal and the 221st was deeply involved.

For this operation, Jim Saller and I were joined by Dennis Clark, a company armorer and friend who wondered what it was like in the bush. So we persuaded the officers to let him join us, learning to shoot motion pictures on the job. A couple of times Tom Wolzien, a good guy and lieutenant, worked with us, providing adult supervision.

Gods Die, Too.

One of the places we stayed from time to time was a huge tent put up for civilian and military journalists on the base at Khe Sanh. One night we shared it with civilian superstars: Larry Burrows of *Life* magazine; Kent Potter of UPI; Henri Huet of AP; Keisaburo Shimamoto of *Newsweek*.

Considering our lowly status, they were very friendly and not in the least bit condescending. We helped them out, sharing some of our warmer gear since it was cold and damp.

That morning, we had hot coffee and ate C-rations for breakfast. I remember Huet being pleased to get pound cake, which most of us considered a special treat. He said something along the lines of "This is going to be my lucky day."

It was not.

As American soldiers, we were forbidden to go into Laos. But getting there was the goal for Burrows and the others. They had a chance to hitch a ride on a Vietnamese Huey and took it. It was a bold move but this was a huge opportunity for a story.

They all died when they were shot down over Laos.

It was pretty grim in the tent that night. It was like gods had died.

Mutiny on Route Nine

During *Dewey Canyon II*, we also moved up and down Route Nine looking for stories. That included working with a troop responsible for patrolling Route Nine and protecting the supply convoys.

One day, part of the troop (we weren't with them) was badly ambushed. In the chaos, they left behind a disabled APC (Armored Personnel Carrier) or two and crews. A Huey came to try and get them and it, too, was shot down. Somehow, another Huey managed to save that crew but left behind the guys from the troop.

We were with the guys working up a plan for a rescue. It involved a "thunder run," which was basically getting a few APCs and volunteers and racing down as quickly as they could to rescue those guys before it got dark, at which time it was thought the NVA would attack.

It was getting towards dusk and they needed volunteers, so I grabbed my M-79 and jumped on one of the tracks, figuring it would be interesting. We raced down with the M-60s and fifty-calibers firing into the jungle alongside the road while I fired my high-explosive rounds. I don't have a good excuse for why I didn't film, other than it seemed more important to be shooting.

We stopped, grabbed those guys and headed back. At one point I heard a whoosh behind me. I figured a rocket-propelled grenade just missed our APC and later a guy in the track behind us confirmed it had been very close. To everyone's amazement we got down and back without anyone being hurt.

But there was still trouble ahead: Mutiny.

Somebody back at headquarters decided it would be bad to allow the NVA to capture the radio in the Huey, which was still sitting down the road. So the order came down to send some APCs there and guard the Huey all night.

Everyone there knew this was a bone-headed plan, since the NVA were dug in down there and we'd fooled them once with the thunder run, but that wasn't going to work again. The guys refused, saying somebody would get killed for no good reason and they should simply have a Cobra or artillery blow up the Huey.

One by one they were asked, and each refused the direct order. It didn't affect us. But we sympathized with the guys from the troop. They were smart and some bozo officer was willing to waste lives for a dumb radio they could just blow up.

The next morning, that troop was to be sent back for some kind of punishment and we headed back to the press tent at Khe Sanh looking for the first civilian reporter we could find to tell about it.

Our thought was some publicity would make it much harder for the Army to screw those guys since it was such an embarrassingly dumb order. We ran into H.D.S. Greenway. His article was called *Incident On Route Nine* and appeared in *TIME* magazine on April 5, 1971.

116   Cameras, Combat and Courage

Nui Coto: In the Delta we spent time with the 9th ARVN Division at a mountain called Nui Coto, a complex of caves and a Viet Cong stronghold.

At one point the ARVN attacked a cave but never managed to get inside. One ARVN was wounded by a ricochet.

Another day the American advisor called in a kind of napalm that was dropped on suspected caves. He's crouching because of a concern about snipers.

Frames from film footage taken by Sp.4 Christopher Jensen, 221st Signal Company

118   *Cameras, Combat and Courage*

Into the A Shau, 1971: In 1971 we went with the 101st on a combat assault into the A Shau Valley. The LZ was the top of a mountain blown off by a huge bomb and there was no opposition.

Then, it was the usual routine. Grunting and straining with lots of heavy gear to work up and down the mountains through a thick tangle of jungle.

There was no contact with the NVA – which did not break anyone's heart – but it was an excellent chance to show just how hard grunts had to work in I Corps.

Frames from film footage taken by Sp.4 Christopher Jensen, 221st Signal Company

Into the A Shau

In the spring of 1971, the 101st Airborne decided to send a company back into the A Shau, typically considered a very bad place if you were an American.

Saller, Clark and I went along.

It started with blowing a landing zone on top of a mountain and then a classic helicopter combat assault. It was a cold landing zone, nobody shooting at us. Then everybody saddled up and headed off into a thick tangle of jungle.

We'd often gone with grunts and we knew just enough about how things worked to know we were very vulnerable. As the afternoon wore along, we ideally should have been on some high ground, setting up a night defensive position, putting out Claymore mines, and arranging for artillery cover in case of an attack.

But instead, we were in a streambed slopping along with steep hills on two sides. We were making a lot of noise and would have been easy pickings for the NVA had they been able to get into position above us. There would have been no place to hide.

Finally it was dark when we were told to make a left turn and head up the hillside. Soon the water from boots and pants created a slick surface so there was even more noise as GIs carrying huge rucksacks slid and fell.

Eventually, I guess, the captain just gave up. We were strung in a line down the hillside. One of us would face one direction and the next guy would flip around and watch the other side. We were one long, vulnerable line. And that is how we stayed.

Happily there were no NVA close or they chose not to attack. The next couple of days were spent patrolling. We shot lots of good film of grunts on patrol and then being lifted out. There was no contact with the NVA.

I often wondered if maybe we had just been bait. Maybe they just wanted to see what happened, and if there was heavy contact they would send in other companies.

Me and Dennis Clark (left); Clark was a company armorer and friend who wanted to experience the bush with us, so we talked some officers into letting him come with us for motion picture on-the-job training.

From Phnom Penh to Ripcord 121

Bits and Pieces*

In fifteen months I was never in what anyone would call a serious firefight. In 1970 and 1971 the war was winding down and maybe I was just lucky. But there were some memories with staying power.

* One night we were at the Khe Sanh base when – just before dawn – we heard explosions. We grabbed our gear and headed across the base as it was getting light.

  On the far perimeter there had been a sapper attack. The sappers had gone after the helicopters parked nearby and damaged a bunch of them, including Cobra attack helicopters. They also blew up some munitions.

  The fighting was over, so we photographed the aftermath, the damaged helicopters, and the bodies of the sappers. One had either blown himself up or a bullet hit an

In the swamps of the U Minh Forest, in the Delta covering ARVN troops. I was constantly trying not to trip over underwater obstacles and dunking my camera.

explosive (satchel) charge on his chest. It wasn't pretty. Then I glanced over, and a dog that was a pet of one of the GIs was nibbling up pieces of the sapper that had been blown off. Bad dog.

* Sometimes we killed ourselves. One late afternoon we were with a cavalry troop and saw three soldiers screaming and carrying a fourth, whose brains were trailing behind. They were trying to find the medic. The dead guy had been trying to unjam an M-60 and it fired.
* One time we were not too far from a Huey sitting idling, waiting to pick up somebody. A mortar hit it. Suddenly the whole thing was in flames with the big rotors still going around and around through the orange and the crew inside.
* The first dead body I saw was largely decomposed. I was with a company of grunts and we came upon it as we moved down a trail in III Corps. We smelled it first. Apparently he'd been killed long before, probably by a gunship. I wasn't careful enough and stepped in a little piece of him that was farther down the trail. The rest of the afternoon my jungle boot smelled of dead guy. I was very careful not to do that again.

Back to the World

By July 1, 1971, I had spent fifteen months in Vietnam. I loved being a photographer and worked with some great people. But my tour was up.

I did consider coming back as a civilian, but thought Vietnam was winding down. It was becoming a very old story and the demand for photos would be slim. There didn't seem to be a future in it and I went home to attend George Washington University as a journalism major.

Now, forty-three years later, I look at Vietnam with a greater depth of field about how badly many of America's young people were used (although I went willingly) by politicians, and how sad it is that so many Vietnamese and Americans were killed and wounded for no good reason.

But I think it was a good thing that photographers from the 221st captured the actions of the young men who went to Vietnam when their country told them. I never thought of us making historical documents but that's what we did. That film and those photos are now in the National Archives.

"... I think it was a good thing that photographers ... captured the actions of the young men who went to Vietnam when their country told them. I never thought of us making historical documents but that's what we did. That film and those photos are now in the National Archives.

*On a mountaintop somewhere in
I Corps, I seem to be showing
an inappropriate exuberance and
energy that suggests hysteria.*

124   Cameras, Combat and Courage

James Saller
Then
U.S. Army
Combat Photographer
221st Signal Company
Long Binh
Republic of Vietnam

"Near Khe Sanh, September, 1970."

Now
Retired
Rochester, New York

Vietnam – Combat Photography 101 – f/8 and Pray

James Saller

On June 7, 1969, I graduated from the Rochester Institute of Technology (RIT) in upstate New York with a Bachelor of Science Degree in professional photography.

Exactly one week later, on June 14, I received my draft notice.

My twin brother, Joe, returned from Vietnam while I was finishing up final exams during my senior year at RIT. He spent a week at our Pennsylvania home before going on to his next duty station in Puerto Rico, so I didn't have a chance to see him then.

Joe was an electrician with the Seabees' 133rd MCB (Mobile Construction Battalion). He worked mostly in the areas around Da Nang and was there for the Tet (Vietnamese Lunar New Year) Offensive of 1968.

My parents were really upset when I received orders for Vietnam. They thought it was unfair that two of their three sons (we have an older brother, John) would have to go to Vietnam.

Later, anytime I was flying out of Da Nang on a mission, I'd have to walk over a concrete slab with the 133rd MCB emblem on it. Also in the cement were the names of the Seabees that had worked on the airport, including Joe's name. So every time I walked out to a plane, I made it a point to step on my brother's name.

Joe's advice to me when he learned I was going to Vietnam was something like, "Keep your head down and don't drink the water."

I entered the Army in August of 1969. My first stop was Fort Jackson, South Carolina, where I completed my Basic training. I left Basic as a private (E-2) and was assigned an 84B50 (Still Photographer) MOS (Military Occupational Specialty) immediately afterwards. I didn't even have to attend the photographic training school at Fort Monmouth, New Jersey, as did so many of the other military photographers I would later meet.

My next duty station was Fort Riley in Kansas. I endured the typical Army process of being sent to a location and being notified that there was no need there for my particular MOS. After arriving at Fort Riley, I was sent to the 138th Engineering Battalion, Headquarters Company. I was sort of stranded there for about two weeks.

One Saturday, the commanding officer, a first lieutenant of the HQ company and I had an informal conversation. He wanted to know how to operate the 35mm Honeywell Pentax camera he had just bought at the PX (Post Exchange – the base store). During the course of this conversation, he asked me about my MOS and my schooling in Rochester.

The following Monday he "loaned" me to the Military Police on the base. I began working for the MPs, taking pictures of accidents, prisoner identification, etc. I had my own desk and a small black and white processing darkroom. I had an account at the PX right across the street to do all of the color processing. It was great duty.

The problem was that I was not officially assigned to the MPs; I was still assigned to the 138th Engineers. And to them I was also considered "additional personnel." That made me available for another assignment.

Soon I received orders for Vietnam.

I arrived there in late May of 1970. My first impression of Vietnam after I exited the plane was the heat and the humidity. On top of the heat and humidity, there was a pungent smell of muddy water, rotting vegetation, and other unknown organic matter.

Chris Jensen snapped me admiring some orchid flowers that I had found.

I went through some in-country training. I think it mostly was the Army's way of getting your body acclimated to the heat. Finally, I was assigned to the 221st Signal Company. I didn't know anyone at the 221st because I didn't go to Fort Monmouth as had most of them. But the next day, I met Ray Linn. Ray was from my home town in Pennsylvania. He showed me around and introduced me to the rest of the guys.

Back home, my camera collection included a Hasselblad, two Nikon Fs and a 4x5 view camera, and multiple lenses for all of them. The 221st supplied me with a Beseler Topcon 35mm and a Graflex XL with a 2-1/4 x 3-1/4 roll film back. I also carried an Asahi Pentax with three lenses – 28mm, 55mm, and 150mm – that I bought at the PX, because I liked the metering system in it.

The first day on the job, I was told to take some pictures around Long Binh. I guess they wanted to know if this "non-army-trained" photographer could take pictures. I must have done alright because the next day I was given the assignment to take

Chris also caught me gnawing on a plastic fork somewhere in the U Minh Forest.

Just a really cool sunset that I caught through the barbed wire when I was in Khe Sanh.

some "grip-and-grins" at USARV (U.S. Army Vietnam) Headquarters. A grip-and-grin is when someone receives a medal or promotion. The awarding officer hands the recipient the citation while shaking their hand while they both smile at the camera.

At one time when I went with the ARVN (Republic of Vietnam Army) to the U Minh Forest I brought along a Leica. I had placed a 200mm lens on it. While sloshing through about three feet of water, I looked down and the lens was no longer on the camera. I had to fill out a "combat loss form" in triplicate for that one. One of the things that I frequently thought of while in Vietnam was how glad I was that I didn't have to pay for all these cameras. I probably ruined a dozen of them. The moisture and dirt and everything else was really rough on the equipment.

Along with my cameras I usually carried a camera cleaning kit, bug repellent, gun oil, three or four pairs of socks, 200 rolls of 35mm film, 50 rolls of 120mm film, the extra lenses for the Pentax, and a book to read whenever.

As far as weapons go I carried a .45 pistol and a M-16. Also, an air mattress, poncho liner, canteens, toothbrush and other personal stuff. No underwear necessary, because you didn't want to walk around with wet undershorts.

One bad experience I had with my kit was that the bug repellent and the gun oil were in very similar plastic bottles. I accidently put gun oil on my face and neck instead of bug repellent. So instead of repelling bugs, the gun oil actually attracted them.

My first field assignment was with the 1st Cavalry during their incursion into Cambodia. I did this assignment solo. I was with the 1st Cav for about a week. While in Cambodia I watched and photographed elephants being used to pull logs. Just like National Geographic.

The infantry would go into villages with some medics. The medics would try to help the injured or sick villagers the best they could with their limited medical resources. I thought this would be a great photo-op. And it was. I took some really interesting pictures.

It was ungodly hot there. I had only been in-country for less than a month and I was really feeling the heat. I had taken my fatigue jacket off and had rolled up my fatigue pants to above my knees. A little Cambodian boy, maybe five or six years old, ran up to me pointing at my exposed legs and yelling "blanc!! blanc!!" The interpreter told me that the child had never seen skin so white.

The 1st Cav captured a large number of guns, light machine guns, mortars, ammo, etc. and uncovered a number of large bunker complexes. I covered all of it. I even tried to take available light photographs inside the bunkers with the aid of two flashlights. The results weren't that good.

The next assignment was to Tay Ninh, where I was asked to photograph a Signal Corps installation. I was there about three days. I slept in an actual bed and had meals in an actual restaurant.

Again, I was on assignment by myself.

Then, in the end of June or early July, I was teamed up with Christopher Jensen. In early July of 1970, Chris, Jerry Dubro (another motion picture shooter) and I went to FSB (Fire Support Base) Ripcord. Ripcord was located on the edge of the A Shau Valley. I believe the intention of the 101st commanders was to place a number of FSBs along the edge of the A Shau to give support to the infantry making search and destroy missions into the valley. But the NVA (North Vietnamese Army) decided to make a stand at and around Ripcord. For about twenty days in July, Ripcord and the infantry companies around it were engaged with a very large number of NVA troops.

While we were there, a 105mm Howitzer gun crew moved their weapon out into the open at the end of one of the landing pads. The NVA were so close that the gun crew had to lower the barrel of the gun all the way down between its tires and push it down the hill a bit so they could fire directly at the lower hillside filled with enemy soldiers. While I was trying to capture a photo of this gun crew in action, I was wounded by incoming rocket fire. I received a Purple Heart and a Bronze Star with Device for my efforts.

Ripcord was evacuated around July 23rd.

After I spent about two or three weeks convalescing, I was back in the field with Chris Jensen, this time in a place called Kham Duc. It is my understanding that Kham Duc was the site of a big battle in 1968. When we arrived at a unit to take pictures, we usually volunteered to pull guard duty. And so it was when we arrived at Kham Duc.

That night, there was an attack on the base. Sappers (NVA commandos) attempted to breach the perimeter almost directly in front of the bunker Chris and I were manning. It seemed like the weapons firing from both sides never stopped. Artillery behind us was firing right over our heads.

At Kham Duc, I still had stitches and bandages from my wounds at Ripcord. Even after being wounded and surviving the sapper attack, I still wanted to capture better combat photographs. I had the feeling more than once while I was in Vietnam, that I wasn't really part of the action. Instead, I felt like an observer of the action, recording it with the film in my cameras. I think other combat photographers felt this as well. It was like watching a news report through the viewfinder.

105mm Howitzer gun crew at Fire Support Base Ripcord during the NVA attack. As the enemy started up the hill, the crew had to lower the gun barrel to where it was now firing between the tires to effectively target them. As I was taking these pictures, an incoming rocket hit near us and I was wounded. For my efforts, I received a Purple Heart and a Bronze Star with a "V" for Valor.

"I had the feeling more than once while I was in Vietnam, that I wasn't really part of the action."

"Instead, I felt like an observer of the action, recording it with the film in my cameras."

"I think other combat photographers felt this as well. It was like watching a news report through the viewfinder."

I always took a lot of photos, so many that to this day, I can still remember the callus I developed on the left side of my right thumb from hitting the film advance lever on my cameras so many times.

The aftermath of this attack was recorded in some stunning and very graphic motion picture footage by Chris. (It eventually made its way to YouTube under Chris' name.)

Early in 1971, Chris and I covered Operation *Lam Son 719*. It mostly involved the South Vietnamese Army going into Laos. We were in I Corps, on and around Khe Sanh.

I was sitting on a pallet on a log-pad (logistics cargo helicopter pad) reading a book while we were waiting for a lift to an infantry unit. There were a lot of ARVN solders milling around. All at once Chris grabbed me and pulled me away from the area. It appeared I was in the line of fire right between two irate ARVN solders that were drawing weapons on each other.

During *Lam Son 719*, we were on Route 9 with an infantry division, the 5th Mechanized, when were we caught in a mortar attack. I sustained permanent partial hearing loss when a mortar shell landed too close to the foxhole I was in.

I also recall shooting a photo of one of the 5th's troopers taking a smoke break in a foxhole. I seem to recall his last name as Carpenter. Goggles on his forehead, he was

This photo of me with my Graflex XL was taken two days before I was wounded at Fire Support Base Ripcord. The camera was "wounded" as well when pieces of shrapnel went through the rangefinder and 100mm lens barrel. I had the camera with me at the Phu Bai evacuation hospital, but I lost track of it after I was transferred to the convalescent center.

132   *Cameras, Combat and Courage*

A few more of the photos I shot at Ripcord. These came from the National Archives, where a lot of our photos can be found today. Most of the time we had no idea of where they were going or if they were even going to be used for anything at all.

CC 70179 111-CCV-626
VIETNAM
A 105mm howitzer battery of the 2nd Bn, 506th Inf, 101st Abn Div, at Fire Support Base "Ripcord."
7-14 July 1970
Photo by SP4 James Saller
221st Sig Co

AVGG-C-8997-3/AGA70
UNCLASSIFIED by USAPA, 30 Nov 70

fn

REVIEWED FOR MILITARY SECURITY
UNCLASSIFIED
NOV 30 1970 (4)
UNITED STATES
ARMY PHOTOGRAPHIC AGENCY
WASHINGTON, D. C. 20310

70179

CC 70186 111-CCV-626
VIETNAM
Members of the 2nd Bn, 506th Inf, 101st Abn Div, stack rounds for their 105mm howitzers at Fire Support Base "Ripcord."
7-14 July 1970
Photo by SP4 James Saller
221st Sig Co

AVGG-C-8997-12/AGA70
UNCLASSIFIED by USAPA, 30 Nov 70

fn

REVIEWED FOR MILITARY SECURITY
UNCLASSIFIED
NOV 30 1970 (4)
UNITED STATES
ARMY PHOTOGRAPHIC AGENCY
WASHINGTON, D. C. 20310

70186

134   Cameras, Combat and Courage

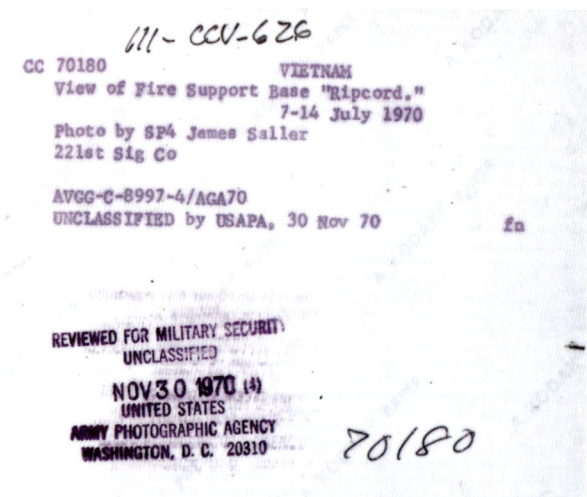

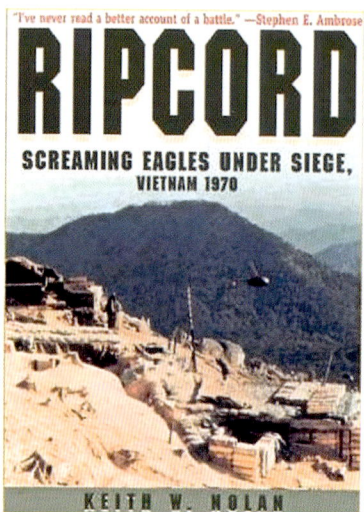

I shot this aerial of Fire Support Base Ripcord in July of 1970, as the caption on the back of the photo shows. It was retrieved from the National Archives and used in a Wikipedia article about Ripcord and a book by Keith Nolan. Like almost all military photographers, we never received credit lines for our photos whenever and wherever they were used. Dan Brookes, the author of *Cameras, Combat and Courage*, edited the Wikipedia page and added my name and information as the photographer.

"Before Kham Duc" picture I shot of (left to right) Larry Brock, Chris Jensen, and John Luckey.

"After Kham Duc" photo of the same three guys, much the worse for wear after the battle. Larry was a still photographer, Chris and John were motion picture. After Kham Duc you could say that we "got the innocence kicked out of us."

136 *Cameras, Combat and Courage*

A trooper with the 5th Infantry Division (Mechanized). As I was photographing him, he just looked back at me with that all-too-common "thousand-yard stare" – the unemotional, detached gaze of a battle-weary soldier. I seem to remember his last name as Carpenter. He was killed in action the following morning.

Left: Dennis Clark, (*right*) a 221st Signal Company mopic (motion picture) shooter, an unidentified trooper, and I were under a mortar attack on Route 9 near the Laotian border with the 5th Infantry. I sustained permanent partial hearing loss when a mortar shell landed near the foxhole. (*Photo by Sp.4 Christopher Jensen, 221st Signal Company*)

Near Khe Sanh on Operation Lam Son 719, members of the 5th Infantry carry a wounded ARVN soldier to a field hospital.

Captured enemy weapons included this anti-aircraft gun. I took this back at the 1st ARVN Division Forward Headquarters.

138 *Cameras, Combat and Courage*

At the Laotian border, an ARVN MP makes sure I stay on the Vietnam side. Technically, we were not allowed to go into Laos at that time. "Technically."

Chris Jensen (*right*) and I take a break at the same border location. Both photos were also during Lam Son 719.

Vietnam – Combat Photography 101 – f/8 and Pray 139

On this mission, I ended up helping the medics treat this guy who was wounded after setting off a boobytrap. I believe we were in II Corps with the 173rd Airborne. That's me in the top part of the first and fourth frames, and on the right in frames five and six. A chopper finally arrived and we got him Medevacked out.

Frames from film footage taken by Sp.4 Christopher Jensen, 221st Signal Company

covered with the grime of battle and looked right at me with that classic "thousand-yard stare." He was killed in action the following morning.

After *Lam Son 719*, on one of my last combat assignments, we were back in the A Shau Valley with the 101st Airborne. They were searching for a downed helicopter that had crashed months earlier. So we're walking up the hill and down the hill and up the hill and down the hill – you get the picture. There just wasn't anything really photogenic in this activity. And besides that, I was getting bone-tired.

Evening came and we set up a night defensive position (NDP). I got some interesting pictures of guys digging foxholes, heating and eating C-rations, talking on the radio, etc. etc. You see, there was always something to photograph. Even routine activity was well worth documenting. At dawn the following morning, I sat up on my air mattress, looked around, and about ten feet front in front of the foxhole was a human skeleton. We had stumbled upon the wreck and didn't even know it until just then. The wrecked helicopter was just down the hill from our NDP location.

In April of 1971, I was assigned to a VIP trip. A two-star general was rotating out of Vietnam and he wanted to make a tour of all the installations under his command. He wanted a photographer along. I became one of his small tour group. We went throughout Vietnam, Thailand, and Hong Kong.

One of our first stops was Cam Ranh Bay. That night, the local commanders held a reception for the general. They really put on a show. Dinner was "surf and turf." For months prior to this assignment I had been out in the field eating C-rations. I got deathly ill after eating all of that rich food.

Every place we stopped, it was the same thing. We would have a tour of the facility. The general would hand out some medals and commendations, and then there was some sort of presentation and the big meal. This went on for two weeks.

Left to right: Me, Chris Jensen, and Dennis Clark. I'm shooting stills, Chris and Dennis are manning their mopic cameras. Chris has a bunch of rounds for his "thumper" M-79 grenade launcher sitting in front of him.

After the VIP trip, I was back in I Corps with the First Division ARVN Rangers. I was with them until the beginning of May. After that, I returned to Long Binh.

My last assignment was to take aerial shots of the Long Binh Jail (LBJ) that was under construction. It was a large stockade for the confinement of military personnel who had violated some aspect of the UCMJ, the Uniform Code of Military Justice.

I left Vietnam at the end of May 1971. Since I was within 90 days of my end of active duty, I was discharged at that time under the "early-out" program. I had served just over twenty-one months.

When I first arrived in Vietnam I had a rather neutral attitude about the war. I really didn't understand why we were fighting. At the time I wasn't all that well-versed in world politics and the "domino theory." All I really wanted to do was take some decent pictures and get home alive.

I was fortunate to have worked alongside some very good photojournalists and photographers. I was really lucky to team up with Chris Jensen and the other talented members of the 221st. It was actually exciting at times. Overall, I felt that my time in Vietnam was well spent.

142   *Cameras, Combat and Courage*

Marvin Wolf
Then
U.S. Army
Combat Photographer
& Information Specialist
1st Cavalry Division
(Airmobile)
Central Highlands
Republic of Vietnam

"*In 1968, two years after completing my combat tour in Vietnam, I became the Information Officer of the Seventh Infantry Division at Tongducheon, ROK.*"

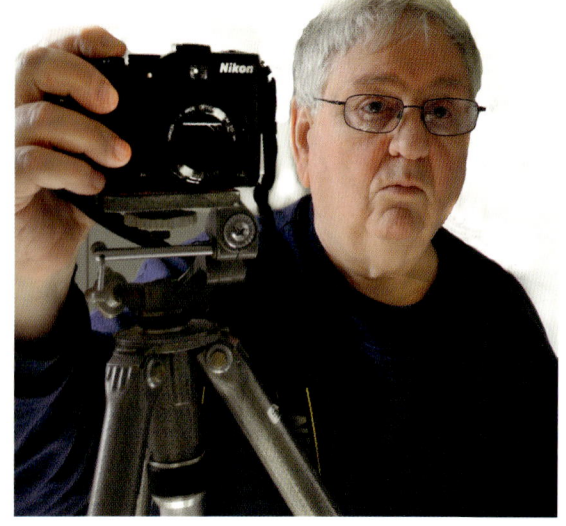

Now
Author
Screenwriter
Photojournalist
Los Angeles, California

Marvin J. Wolf

I grew up in Chicago and moved with my family to Los Angeles in 1957. After graduating high school in February 1959, I enlisted in the US Army and took Basic and Advanced Infantry Training at Fort Ord, California. There I earned the Expert Infantryman's Badge. After completing my training, I was assigned to a Fourth Infantry Division rifle company at Fort Lewis, Washington.

At Fort Lewis, I served as a platoon leader's RTO before attending the post NCO Academy. I graduated second in my class and was promoted to the rank of specialist four. In February 1960, I was selected as the Fort Lewis Soldier of the Month.

In March I was transferred to a rifle company in the Seventh Infantry Division in the Republic of Korea. I served first as a machine gun team leader and, after promotion to sergeant, as weapons squad leader. Upon completion of my overseas tour in 1961, I was reassigned to Fort Benning, Georgia, where I joined the Infantry School's Ranger Combat Conditioning Committee. During the Berlin Wall crisis of late 1961, I served as a Basic training drill instructor at Fort Jackson, South Carolina. I was discharged in April 1962.

After returning to civilian life, I worked in sales. Since childhood, I had been an avid amateur photographer, and subsequently became interested in photojournalism.

Goofing around with a girl weaving straw for roof thatch in An Khe.

A First Cav medic administers a saline drip to a wounded warrior.

A platoon from Alpha Battery 2/20 Aerial Rocket Artillery delivers a salvo on an NVA position east of Bong Son.

Without funds to attend college, I decided to re-enlist, hoping to receive on-the-job training in that field. After re-enlisting as a private in March 1965, I returned to Fort Benning.

En route by car to Fort Benning, I drove through Selma, Alabama on the day when a massive civil rights demonstration led by the Reverend Martin Luther King, Jr. took place. I stopped to photograph it.

Later, my photos of that demonstration attracted the attention of the Second Infantry Division information officer. After two months in a rifle company, I was given on-the-job-training as an information specialist. In practice, this meant having to find visual stories and photograph them with little guidance from anyone. After sixty days of self-training, I was awarded military occupational specialty 71Q – Information Specialist.

The following day, the Second Infantry Division at Fort Benning was redesignated The First Cavalry Division (Airmobile) and merged with the 11th Air Assault Division (TEST), whose colors were retired. (The Second Infantry Division colors were sent to the Republic of Korea and the former units of the First Cavalry Division were re-designated as Second Infantry Division units.)

I was promoted to private first class and deployed with the advance party of the First Cavalry, arriving in Vietnam in late August 1965. There I played a small but vital role in the advance party's key mission by going aloft in a helicopter to make low-oblique photographs of the previously uncharted area that would become the division base, Camp Radcliff.

From August to May 1966, I spent most of my time in the field, photographing combat operations and learning the rudiments of news writing. Following my promotion to sergeant in May 1966, I served as press chief of a greatly expanded Public Information Section. My duties encompassed supervising all information specialists, including those assigned as photographers, and managing the section's work flow of news and photographic releases. I was also designated to escort visiting journalists, including, most notably, John Steinbeck and the noted military historian S.L.A. Marshall.

My Vietnam tour was involuntarily extended through November 1966, when I was commissioned a second lieutenant of infantry, one of some sixty American soldiers and marines to earn a commission in the field during the Vietnam War.

Over the next eight years I served in a variety of staff and command positions, including company commander, battalion adjutant and as the Information Officer of the Seventh Infantry Division at Tongducheon, Republic of Korea. I left active duty as a captain in August 1974.

* * *

Editor's Note: *After a few years in corporate communications jobs, Wolf struck out on his own and has been self-employed since 1978. After a decade working primarily as a photojournalist, he segued into writing. Wolf is the author of hundreds of magazine and newspaper feature and news stories and a dozen nonfiction books under his own name, as well as several others written as a ghost. His 2005 screenplay,* Ladies Night, *based on a true story from one of his own books, was produced as a two-hour television movie that aired on the USA Network.*

In 2011 Wolf turned to fiction. The Tattooed Rabbi *was the first of the Rabbi Ben series. The second,* The YouTube Rabbi, *was published late in 2012, and he has begun work on other novels.*

On the following pages is Marv's retelling of one of his more memorable missions in Vietnam.

Our Friendly Neighborhood VC Sniper

Marvin J. Wolf

The bullet landed in the rice paddy in front of me. I never heard a shot; my first inkling was the fountain of muddy water spouting from the paddy to cover me with filth.

I went headfirst into the paddy, the big, boxy Speed Graphic camera held straight out in front of me.

As far as I know, it's still there.

It's weird, what I was thinking, soaking in a foot of filthy water as a few seconds ticked by before the rifle platoon from Second Battalion, Twelfth Cavalry, returned fire.

Later, on the flight back to base camp, I would reflect on that moment and realize that we were fifty-plus men in four columns, dressed identically—but I was the only one carrying a big, black box. And that a tiny adjustment of the sniper's sights, perhaps a click or two on the elevation knob, would have put that bullet in me instead of the paddy.

But right then, at the moment that I found myself in muddy water, I was thinking, Thank God, that effing monstrosity of a camera is finished. It was heavy and awkward to carry in the field. Two hands and five separate actions were required to make each exposure, not including composing the shot. Its 25-year-old viewfinder was cloudy and its wire "sports finder" imprecise.

And at our base camp, just then a collection of tents with dirt floors and repurposed CONEX containers—steel shipping boxes sunk into the ground and covered with sandbags—we had no easy way to process 4x5-inch sheet film. Developing it required swishing one or two sheets at a time through trays of chemicals in total darkness in a stifling, airless, makeshift darkroom where daytime temperatures reached 140 degrees. Our enlarger couldn't handle film that big; we made do with contact prints.

It was such a hassle, took so much of my time, that I sent our raw film to the division signal battalion's photo section, where the average turn-around time ran upwards of a week. I wasn't shooting news photos. I was shooting historical documentation.

Prone in that paddy, I was thinking not only how glad I was that the Graphic was ruined, but also that a week earlier Henri Huet, an AP photographer, had taken my hundred dollars to Japan and bought me a Nikonos, a waterproof 35mm camera. It was in my butt back.

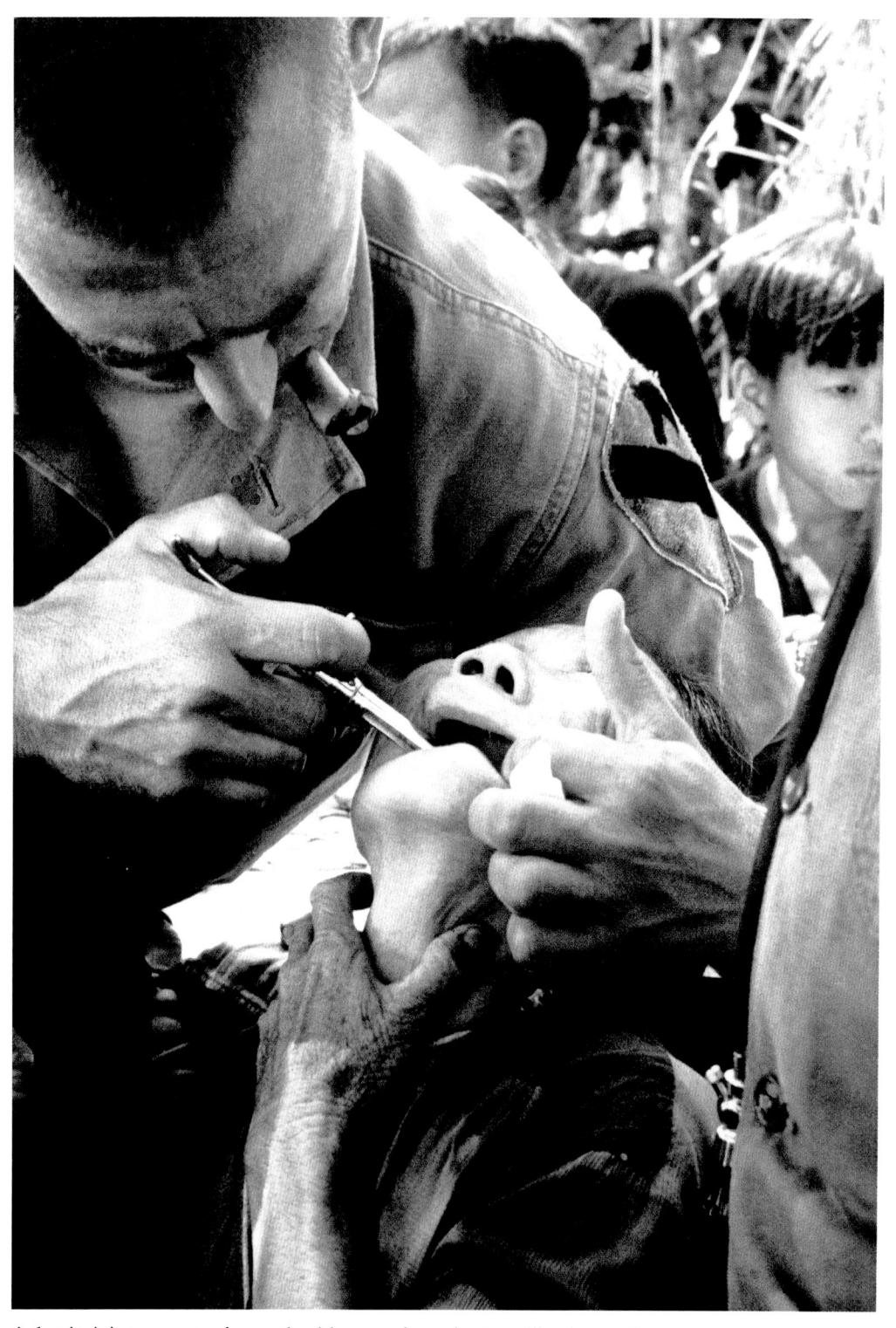

A dentist injects a woman's mouth with novocaine prior to pulling her tooth.

Our Friendly Neighborhood VC Sniper   149

Ten seconds, give or take, after I hit the mud, our guys started shooting into a bamboo thicket 200 yards upslope from the narrow, twisting skein of paddies we had been crossing. I looked up in time to see a guy in black pajamas and a conical hat bolt from the thicket. Forty rifles followed him as he dashed down the hill and across a shallow river, bullets splashing all around him, tracers skipping off the water. An M-79 bloop gun coughed behind me and after a few seconds a 40 mm grenade exploded on the far bank. The sniper fell face-first onto a sand bar in midstream.

"Cease fire!" yelled the platoon sergeant. I climbed out of the paddy and stripped off my clothes. A helpful medic with a lighted cigarette burned off six or seven leeches, already swollen with my blood, that had attached themselves to various parts of my body.

While that was in progress, a squad went to retrieve the black pajamas.

They returned with a tiny, wizened old man with a sparse white goatee. Exhausted and shaking with fright, he was otherwise unhurt; not one of the hundreds of shots fired at him had found its target. A couple of riflemen searched the bamboo thicket, returning with a single-shot, bolt-action rifle with a spent cartridge in its chamber. Our sniper turned out to be a grandfather with a World War I-vintage rifle and a single round of ammo. A couple of Vietnamese police were with us, but when they tried to question our prisoner they couldn't make out what he said because his upper lip was cleft in two, a birth defect, and his slow speech was unintelligible.

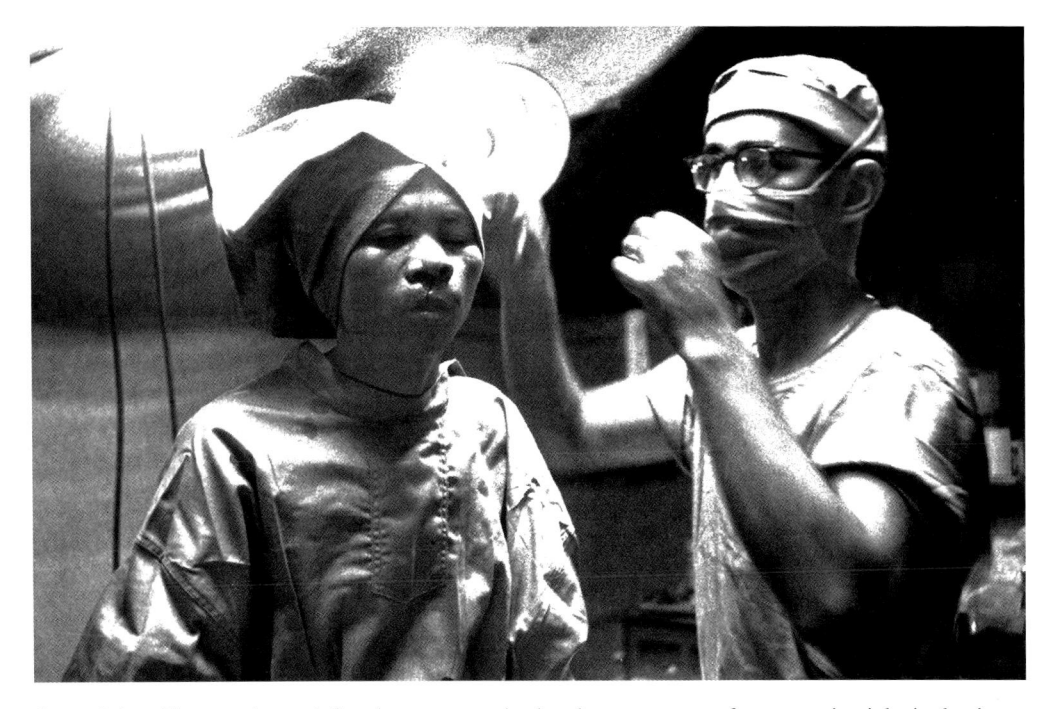

One of the villagers whose cleft palate was repaired as he comes out of surgery. At right is the Army doctor who performed the surgery.

150 *Cameras, Combat and Courage*

A month after I photographed him in surgery, the villager who was operated on smokes his first cigar. To his right is his grandson, whose cleft palate was also repaired.

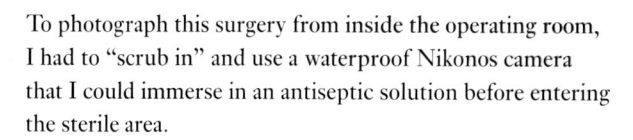

To photograph this surgery from inside the operating room, I had to "scrub in" and use a waterproof Nikonos camera that I could immerse in an antiseptic solution before entering the sterile area.

But this disabled old man had accomplished his purpose. By the time we reached our objective, a hamlet in a narrow valley farther up the river, every man of military age had taken his leave.

Our mission, however, was not to search or destroy but to win hearts and minds. This was a medical civic action program, or MEDCAP, mission. The infantry platoon escorted half a dozen medical corpsmen, two doctors and two dentists. The medics passed out little parcels of antiseptic soap, wash clothes, band aids, sterile dressings, vials of tincture of iodine, tubes of tooth paste, tooth brushes, one packet for every man, woman and child. Basic stuff, but for this remote mountain hamlet, it was more valuable than gold. Many of the kids here would die of infections from cuts or scrapes before they were old enough to start a family of their own. Every adult in the village and most of the older children had at least one tooth that needed attention, and their gums were in terrible shape. Every adult woman's teeth were stained a deep red, almost black, from years of chewing betel nuts to numb their painful teeth.

We held sick call at one end of the village square and dental call at the other. Teeth were pulled, cavities filled. Cuts were stitched and bandaged. Infections were treated with antibiotics. Through translators, doctors diagnosed individual ailments and handed out an assortment of pills and other medicine. As we were packing our gear to leave, a woman went into labor; an Army trauma surgeon delivered her baby.

But the most important thing about this village, it's singular quality and the reason that we came here, rather than to any of a thousand other, equally poor and squalid settlements, was that more than half the males, children and adults, had a cleft palate.

Our medical battalion commander, a physician, had learned of this place from a South Vietnamese colleague and had sent doctors to make friends and earn the villagers' trust.

A few weeks later, a surgical team fortified with resources provided by the United States Agency for International Development and protected by another infantry platoon, returned to the village. I accompanied them, along with my friend and colleague, PFC James Lull, a First Air Cavalry PIO reporter.

Packing our gear out of the LZ a mile from the village, another sniper took a shot at us. We fired back, but he disappeared into the jungle.

The villagers, however, seemed friendly enough. While a State Department anthropologist took family histories from everyone in the village, we set up back-packed gasoline-powered electrical generators and erected an air-conditioned tent that became a surgical theater. Over seven hours, two surgeons repaired some thirty cleft palates on boys as young as three and men as old as sixty, including our grandpa sniper and several young men who had hurriedly left town shortly before our first visit.

A month later we returned for a patient follow up. The neighborhood sniper was waiting near our pick-up LZ. We didn't even bother to return fire.

Corporal William T. Perkins Jr.

United States Marine Corps Combat Photographer

On October 12, 1967 during Operation *Medina* in the Hai Lang Forest in Quang Tri Province, Republic of Vietnam, Cpl. Perkins made the ultimate sacrifice when he hurled himself upon an enemy hand grenade to save the lives of his fellow Marines.

Bill Perkins Jr. is the only combat photographer in U.S. history to receive the Medal of Honor, the nation's highest award for valor.

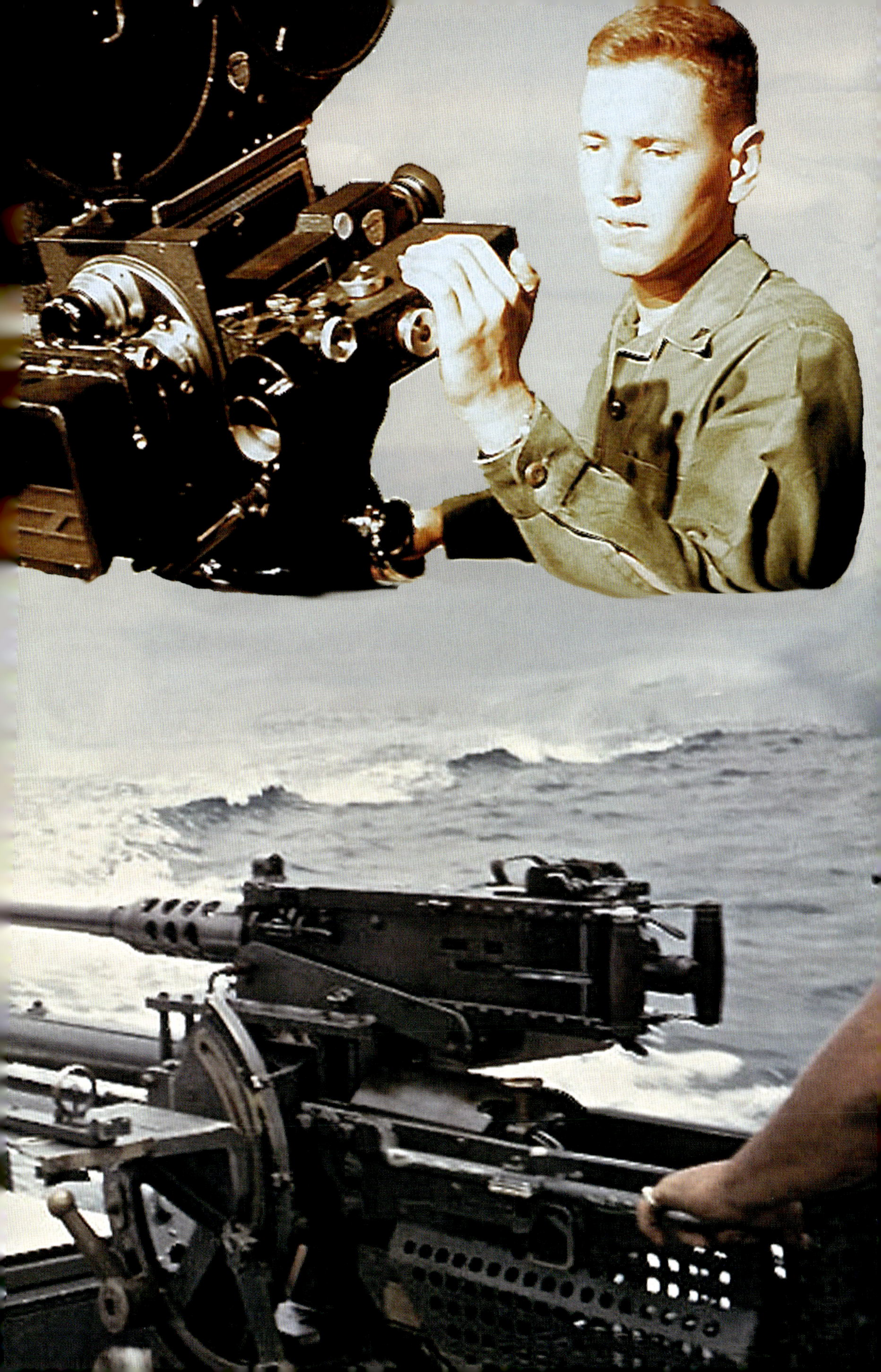

Above and Beyond: The Story of Cpl. William T. Perkins, Jr. USMC

Craig Ingraham

*"The Brave Ones Fought with Weapons.
The Crazy Ones Fought with Cameras."*

Editor's Note: *Thirty years after Cpl. Perkins' death in Vietnam, his friend Craig Ingraham set out on a journey to discover what happened that day in the Hai Lang Forest. Along the way, he discovered so much more. As a result he made the documentary* Above and Beyond: The Story of Cpl. William T. Perkins, Jr. USMC. *It is a fine tribute to a friend and hero by a talented and dedicated musician, writer and filmmaker.*

My Quest to Tell Bill's Story

In 1965, none of us could find Vietnam on a map, but Bill and I found Cal-Aquatics in Woodland Hills, California. We fell in love with scuba diving watching Lloyd Bridges in *Sea Hunt* every Friday night.

Incredible. We fell in love with the ocean and scuba diving. Bill and I became certified SCUBA divers together and spent many hours diving off the southern California coast. Bill was even wearing his dive watch when he was killed during Operation *Medina*.

Bill was intelligent and talented. He was handsome and charismatic. In high school, Bill had the lead role in the play *The Mouse That Roared.* He played Nana the dog in the Valley Music Theater production of *Peter Pan,* starring Janet Blair as Peter Pan and Vincent Price as Captain Hook.

He had a great sense of humor. Bill made you laugh. It is remarkable how many of his fellow Marines in Vietnam smiled and even chuckled as Bill filmed them. He was an American teenager who documented the Vietnam War through his own eyes and became extraordinary in a moment of ultimate sacrifice. He was a United States Marine.

Bill and I met in our junior year of high school in 1964 through our mutual friend Jim Priddy. The three of us shared a twisted sense of humor and spent many hours learning comedy and theater routines together, always laughing and having a great time.

Above and Beyond: The Story of Cpl. William T. Perkins, Jr. USMC 155

The first time I remember talking about the military with Bill was when we were taking our dive classes. Bill spoke of joining a UDT (Underwater Demolition Team), the forerunners of the Navy Seals – swimming into enemy harbors, attaching explosives to enemy ships and getting the hell out of there before you were detected. What could be more macho or patriotic? But actually, Bill wanted to shoot motion pictures more than he wanted to blow up enemy ships. He had already started experimenting with underwater photography.

I had been out on the road playing music for much of 1965 and 1966. I was living with my parents and had no direction. The Vietnam War was in full swing. Every day Americans were dying there with no end in sight.

It had been a while since I had seen Bill and Jim Priddy. Then one morning while I was mowing the lawn I looked up and saw them coming up the street in Bill's old black Volvo. They turned into our circle driveway as I was trying to start the lawnmower. They got out and walked towards me.

They were dressed in white T-shirts and tight blue jeans – part of the "uniform" of that period. One of them said, "Hey Ingraham, guess what we did?"

"What?" I answered.

"We joined the Marines."

"Yeah, right, sure you did," I replied, incredulous.

"No man, we really did!"

I couldn't believe what I was hearing. It shook me to my core. I felt woozy. Before I could say another word, I suddenly had a premonition. It felt like I had been shot through the heart with a diamond. I knew one of them would die in Vietnam. As I looked at them in disbelief, I began to catch my breath. To this day, I can't remember what happened after that. (Little did I know that nearly forty years later, Bill's father would tell me about his own premonition of his son's death while watching the movie *Doctor Zhivago*.)

Before getting on the bus that would take them to the Marine Corps Recruit Depot in San Diego, they were smiling and joking with their families and each other. They looked casual as they seemed to laugh it off. Soon it would be no joke.

Jim recently told me that when they arrived in San Diego, they were told by the drill instructor that the last one off the bus would get the shit kicked out of them. And sure enough, the last kid off the bus was beaten senseless by the drill instructors. Now they were scared. But a drill instructor's job was to make them hard, to make them disciplined, to teach them to take pain, to make them Marines.

When Bill and Jim graduated from Boot Camp, they were Marines, but they weren't laughing quite so hard and the look in their eyes – was trepidation. They had joined the Marines in 1966. Nearly 7,000 Americans had been killed and over 37,000 had been wounded between 1960 and 1966. However in 1967 alone, over 11,000 were killed

Now full-fledged Marines, Bill Perkins (left) and Jim Priddy.

in action and 56,000 were wounded. Vietnam was a dangerous place and that's where my friends were headed.

After graduation from Basic training, Bill was stationed in Barstow, California. He hated it. As his father, Bill Perkins Sr. described in his interview for the documentary, Bill told him that all he did was run around taking pictures of generals and their families. His dream was to shoot motion pictures in Hollywood, to be a cinematographer.

So the Marine Corps made a deal with him. They would send him to mo-pic school at Fort Monmouth, New Jersey. But when he graduated, he would be sent to Vietnam.

The last time I saw Bill, we had a terrible fight. We never spoke again; I am sure that this has driven me to tell his story.

In November 1967, I was attending Pierce College and playing rock 'n roll with my band. I came home from class one afternoon and my Mom said, "I have some bad news for you."

For some reason, I knew. "It's Bill, isn't it?" I said. She handed me the local newspaper and there was Bill's picture in his dress uniform, with the caption "Local Marine Dies in Vietnam."

I couldn't believe it even though I knew it was true. I was so angry. I found a small bottle of Johnnie Walker scotch in the kitchen cabinet. I took it out to the backyard and sat down in the weeds. I unscrewed the top off the bottle and began drinking it down. I hated alcohol but I did it anyway. I drank it down.

* * *

I had always wondered about the circumstances surrounding Bill's death and his recommendation for the Medal of Honor. I knew he had wrapped himself around a hand grenade to save his fellow Marines, but that was all I knew. So, in the early '90s, I started doing research. It was an arduous task since everything was done by phone and mail at that time.

It took some time, but I finally procured copies of the nineteen reels of color motion picture footage that Bill shot in Vietnam. I then found the command chronology for the 1st Battalion, 1st Marines for Operation *Medina* and the eyewitness accounts used to verify his Medal of Honor status.

In 2003, I contacted Ed "Rowdy" Yates, the webmaster of the Charlie Company 1st/1st Marines website. He was understandably skeptical of me at first but gradually I won his trust. He invited me to the 1st Marines reunion in Washington, D.C. to meet the men of Operation *Medina* in August, 2003. Eventually, with the help of the internet and my co-producer Debora Masterson, my dream of telling Bill's story on film was becoming a reality.

Operation *Medina* – The Ultimate Sacrifice

On October 12, 1967, Bill was a twenty-year-old Marine corporal in Vietnam. He was a combat photographer attached to Company C, 1st Battalion, 1st Marine Division on a helicopter headed for Operation *Medina*, a battalion-sized reconnaissance in the Hai Lang forest near the DMZ. They were flown out on helicopters to the edge of the jungle where they jumped out, formed up and began marching into what would soon become hell.

The choppers took off and disappeared. They humped their way through the jungle, walking and chopping through the thick foliage. They crossed a wild, freezing river with one hand on a rope, the other hand holding their weapons above their heads. "I had no idea the river would be that deep and that cold," said Gunnery Sgt. Ron Pelkey. They came to a trail already cut through the jungle. They were given orders to head up the trail.

As Mike Robinson tells it, "The word came back to me and I told the lieutenant, this isn't right, but they told us to go anyway." As they walked up that narrow trail with jungle on both sides, they all knew something was wrong, they could feel it. Sure enough, minutes later, they were ambushed.

Their point man Kevin Cahill had a premonition about Operation *Medina* and it wasn't good. As the bullets flew down the trail towards Company C, Kevin Cahill became the first man killed on Operation *Medina*. That first attack was a short, vicious portent of things to come.

They finally reached a flat area that would become a landing zone. They cleared the area and established a perimeter. Ron Coss told us, "I turned to J.J. and said, 'Man, this is going to be a bad place to be.'"

On the evening of October 12, 1967, fighting raged in and around the LZ held by Company C. They were 165 men outnumbered at least 3 to 1. "The second attack came about 5 or 5:30," said Steve Kane. "As day turned to night, the attack became more and more intense."

"The NVA opened up with everything they had. It was chaos, madness," explained Dennis Antal. He would soon become one of the men whose lives were saved by Bill.

"They were up in the trees inside our perimeter, throwing hand grenades down on us," said George Dougherty. "The spooky thing was that they were American hand grenades. Night was falling and things were getting worse. I knew I was going to die. Just pick who you're gonna die with, try to get with a buddy," he continued.

Joe "JJ" Zorn recalls, "I had a 3.5 rocket launcher and they told you when you're in that kind of situation, when you're being overrun, you destroy the 3.5. So I put it down and kicked the sights out. I found a dead Marine's M-16 and that's how we fought the rest of the night."

Mike Cole recounts, "I had a concussion grenade go off next to me and it blew me over the hill and my feet were just in front of them (NVA)." He managed to get back up the hill. Men were crying for their mothers, crying for water, screaming from the pain. They were running out of everything, including bullets and morphine. Men were dying and many more were wounded but they fought valiantly because they were Marines.

"We were all in a prone position, lying down when the grenade came in," Dennis Antal says with tears in his eyes. "It came up about six or seven feet above us and dropped down on us. It had such a high arc, you could see it silhouetted. It seemed like it took forever (to fall)."

"I looked over and Bill was in a crouching position, kinda on his knees." Dennis chokes up. "He landed on the grenade." Dennis takes a long pause to compose himself. "He didn't have to, he could have gotten down."

Fellow combat photographer Frank Lee said, "When someone like Bill makes that instant decision to try and save someone and dies for that, you have to acknowledge that person for that act."

Still holding his motion picture camera, Bill wrapped himself around the grenade, absorbing the blast with his body, shielding his fellow Marines from the explosion. He saved the lives of his fellow comrades at the cost of his own. When asked what Bill means to him, Dennis Antal doesn't hesitate, "Life… Bill is life to me."

I am often asked what my motivation was in making the documentary and what I hope it will accomplish. My motivation was to find out what really happened to Bill that terrible day in Vietnam. Did he really throw himself on a hand-grenade? What time of day was it? Who was there? Who saw it happen? There was much confusion about his death in that chaotic situation. I got the answers to my questions and much more.

I hope to bring some peace to the hearts of those of us who knew him. I also hope that people who see the film will understand that war is hell for everyone involved. The parents of dead Vietnamese soldiers grieve as deeply as did Bill's mom and dad. It is unnatural for parents to outlive their children. It is a tragedy. I am grateful that Bill's mom and dad were able to see my film. I know that it brought them joy and a bit of solace in the face of unspeakable, unending pain – the death of one's child. Finally, it's my way of acknowledging how profoundly Bill has affected so many lives and that we all love him and miss him.

As I was writing this, the most amazing thing happened. I received a phone call from Jim Priddy in Redmond, Washington. He said that he had spent a week camping in California with a few dozen of his wife's family members and friends. Beer, whiskey and horseshoes.

They were sitting around the fire one night asking each other what their favorite Vietnam War movie was. Of course, the usual suspects were named: *Apocalypse Now*,

(continued on page 168)

160   Cameras, Combat and Courage

The photos that follow are actual film frames and commentary from Craig Ingraham's documentary, *Above and Beyond: The Story of Cpl. William T. Perkins, Jr. USMC*. It has aired on PBS and is available on DVD.

"When he was over there … a movie came out (Doctor Zhivago) … there's a scene in there, they're (soldiers) all out there in the field, all lined up, it was a beautiful fall day, there was like a wheat field … and (two bodies) they're

"Mass was on the tarmac … a Catholic priest said 'It doesn't matter what denomination you are, you can attend Mass.' One Marine made the comment, 'This is gonna be bad, they're giving us our last rites.' Operation Medina was the worst. On a scale of one to ten, it was a twelve. When I saw Bill with his camera, I thought, well, how bad could this be? Because I didn't know how a

Operation Medina – *The Ultimate Sacrifice* 161

laying there ... with all the blood and so forth, and I had a premonition. I saw my son laying in that wheat field, and I couldn't shake it, I just couldn't get it out of my mind."

combat photographer would actually go into combat. When we came to the river ... it was raging, it was swift ... the lieutenant said, 'Hang on to the rope and go. We came to this trail ... I don't think we was on that trail for maybe twenty minutes or a half-hour, then we got ambushed."

"It was chaos, madness. It was so intense we started falling back to make a tighter perimeter ... a minute later everybody was firing." – Dennis Antal

"That's when I called in ... they made the decision at that time to go up this trail. I told the lieutenant, 'This isn't right ... I've got a feeling' but they told us to go anyway. Kevin Cahill was the point man ... he had that premonition

"And then we broke contact, we set up a perimeter, we set up an LZ and called in for the choppers. After the first firefight everyone knew this was gonna be bad."

"I turned to JJ and said, 'Man, this is going to be a bad place to be."

twice (about Operation Medina) and both times he was right but this time he got killed, and he was the first one to leave this land on that operation."

"I think it was about 5:30 when the second attack happened just before dusk."

"It was chaos, madness. It was so intense we started falling back to make a tighter perimeter ... a minute later everybody was firing."

"Night was falling and things were getting worse. I knew I was going to die. Just pick who you're gonna die with, try to get with a buddy." – George Dougherty

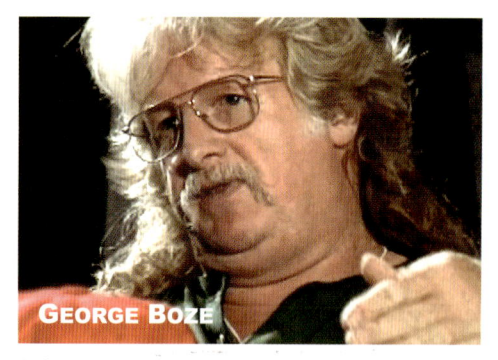

"Off to the left ... where we saw the chopper come in, that's where they made the third assault ... that's where we threw the tear gas down."

"They were up in the trees inside our perimeter, throwing hand grenades down on us ... Night was falling and things were getting worse.

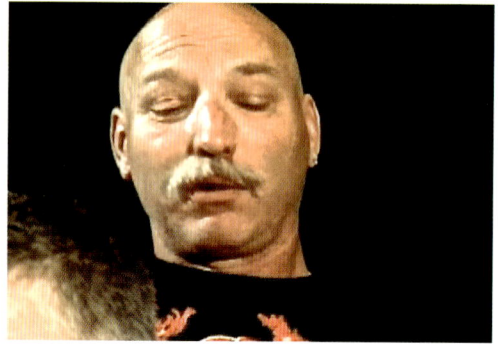

"I had a 3.5 rocket launcher and they told you when you're ... being overrun, you destroy the 3.5. So I put it down and kicked the sights out. I found a dead Marine's M-16 and that's how we fought the rest of the night."

Operation Medina – *The Ultimate Sacrifice* 165

I knew I was going to die. Just pick who you're gonna die with, try to get with a buddy."

"… *they had him (enemy soldier) wrapped on a tree limb with this rope and he was throwing them (grenades) down on top of us."*

"I had a concussion grenade go off next to me and it blew me over the hill and my feet were just in front of them. I crawled to my right and then came back up on to that area."

"You're hearing chaos in the perimeter and you're hearing men crying for their mothers, people calling for their wives, people are dying." – J.J. Zorn

"You're hearing chaos in the perimeter and you're hearing men crying for their mothers, people calling for their wives, people are dying, corpsman asking for water … running out of morphine … running out of ammo."

"So we was all in a prone position, laying down, and when the grenade came in it kinda went up six or seven feet above us. It had such a high arc you could actually see it silhouetted … I think somebody behind me yelled 'grenade' … I looked up and Bill was in a crouching position and kind of on his knees … he

"Bill was in front of me … it was full-out unbelievable firing … explosions. They had us outnumbered and were gonna do their best to wipe us out … I ran out … fired everything I had … I remember Bill threw me a magazine."

landed on the grenade … he didn't have to – he could've gotten down. I put my hand on Bill, and Fred was saying, 'How is he, how is he?' I rolled him over and this (waves hands over chest) was all gone. Bill is to me, one word – life. That's how I would describe it. Bill was life to me."

168   Cameras, Combat and Courage

"For me as a combat cameraman what war does – it squeezes life into one real tight timeframe where twelve months can go by in a flash when you're alive one moment and dead the next. When someone like Bill makes that instant decision to try and save someone and dies for that … you have to acknowledge that person for that act."

— Frank Lee, Combat Cameraman, 3rd Marine Division

"Somebody was on the PA and says, 'Bill Perkins will you please come to the phone, you have a phone call from the White House.' And so I went over to the phone and he says, 'I just found out that your son's been awarded the Medal' … and that's how I first found out about it."

— Bill Perkins Sr., Bill's Father

Platoon, Full Metal Jacket, The Deer Hunter, etc. Then a young man, twenty-four years old, who Jim had just met, told the group that his favorite Vietnam movie was a documentary that he had seen on PBS about a Marine Corps combat photographer who had died throwing himself on a hand-grenade to save the lives of his comrades and received the Medal of Honor for his action.

Jim's mind was blown. He said to the young man, "Do you remember that he joined the Marines with a friend?"

Craig Ingraham
High School friend of Bill's

"The kid was in shock. He told Jim how he had been moved to tears watching the documentary. A twenty-four year-old kid, two generations removed from the Vietnam War, and yet he understood."
"It's for moments like this that I made the film."

"Yes," the young man replied.

"Well," said Jim, "that friend is me."

The kid was in shock. He told Jim how he had been moved to tears watching the documentary. A twenty-four year-old kid, two generations removed from the Vietnam War, and yet he understood. It's for moments like this that I made the film.

Corporal William T. Perkins, Jr.
United States Marine Corps

This photo of Bill's has always touched me deeply.

I've often wondered what that Marine was thinking
as the sun was going down
and Bill was shooting the picture.

Like the photograph, Vietnam was mysterious

Operation Medina – *The Ultimate Sacrifice* 171

Bill Perkins Jr.'s Bell & Howell Eyemo camera that he was filming with when he threw himself on the NVA grenade. The camera is now part of the exhibits at the National Museum of the Marine Corps in Triangle, Virginia.

172   *Cameras, Combat and Courage*

Above right: Perkins (in the red-outlined inset and upper left photo) filming the evacuation of wounded Marines just two hours before he was killed in action. Photograph by Staff Sergeant Bruce Martin, USMC.
Below: President Richard Nixon presents Perkins' Medal of Honor to his parents.

Bill is the only combat photographer in our nation's history to receive the Medal of Honor, our nation's highest award for valor.

Here is Bill's official Medal of Honor citation ratified by Congress and signed by then President Richard M. Nixon.

Citation

The PRESIDENT OF THE UNITED STATES takes pride in presenting the MEDAL OF HONOR posthumously to:

CORPORAL WILLIAM T. PERKINS, JR. UNITED STATES MARINE CORPS

for service as set forth in the following citation:

For conspicuous gallantry and intrepidity at the risk of his life above and beyond the call of duty while serving as a combat photographer attached to Company C, First Battalion, First Marines, First Marine Division, in the Republic of Vietnam on 12 October 1967.

During Operation *MEDINA*, a major reconnaissance in force, southwest of Quang Tri, Company C made heavy combat contact with a numerically superior North Vietnamese Army Force estimated at from two to three companies. The focal point of the intense fighting was a helicopter landing zone which was also serving as the Command Post of Company C.

In the course of a strong hostile attack, an enemy grenade landed in the immediate area occupied by Corporal Perkins and three other Marines. Realizing the inherent danger, he shouted the warning, "Incoming Grenade" to his fellow Marines, and in a valiant act of heroism, hurled himself upon the grenade absorbing the impact of the explosion with his own body thereby saving the lives of his comrades at the cost of his own.

Through his exceptional courage and inspiring valor in the face of certain death, Corporal Perkins reflected great credit upon himself and the Marine Corps and upheld the highest traditions of the United States Naval Service. He gallantly gave his life for his country.

/S/ RICHARD M. NIXON

ghostriders 079

> "On May 9, 1970, five 221st combat photographers were killed in the downing of a UH-1D Huey of the 189th Assault Helicopter Company, GhostRiders 079. The shootdown occurred near Pleiku as the men were taking part in the Cambodian incursion then underway."
> – Paul Berkowitz, 221st Sig. Co. 1st Lt. Team Leader Jul 69-Mar 70

Left to right: Douglas Itri, Raymond Paradis, Larry Young, Christopher Childs, and Ron Lowe. These five Army combat photographers died when their helicopter was shot down near Pleiku, South Vietnam, May 9, 1970. – © 2010 Ken Grissom

Helicopter UH-1D 65-10079

Information on U.S. Army helicopter UH-1D tail number 65-10079
The Army purchased this helicopter 0866
Total flight hours at this point: 00002379
Date: 05/09/70
Incident number: 70050911.KIA
Unit: 189 AHC
South Vietnam
UTM grid coordinates: ZA804436
Original source(s) and document(s) from which the incident was created or updated: Defense Intelligence Agency Helicopter Loss database. Also: OPERA (Operations Report.)
Loss to Inventory

Crew Members:
AC WO1 MCCLUSKEY JOHN DAVID KIA
P 1LT HURD COLIN PLUMMER KIA
CE SP4 FULTON JOHNNY LEE KIA
G PFC CORPUS DAVID JOSEPH KIA

Passengers:
 SP5 CHILDS CHRISTOPHER J III KIA
 SP5 ITRI DOUGLAS JOHN KIA
 SP4 LOWE RONALD SIDNEY KIA
 PFC PARADIS RAYMOND LOUIS KIA
 SP4 YOUNG LARRY CLAYTON KIA

– From the Status Reports and Mission Logs
of the 189th Assault Helicopter Company.

"Combat Photography Was Our Mission"

Paul Berkowitz

Any veterans of the 221st Signal Company (Pictorial), who were there at the time, or who knew any of those lost, can remember exactly where they were when they first heard about *Ghostriders 079*. I was home. I had been home nearly two months and was technically still on "emergency leave." My parents had been critically injured in an auto accident. I was still on active duty, reassigned to Fort MacArthur in San Pedro, California. I wasn't going back. Captain Bill Kelly, bless him, had made sure of that. I would be discharged in a few more weeks. That's when I got word.

I heard it first on the *CBS Evening News*. Nine men had been killed in a helicopter shootdown near Pleiku, five of them Army photographers. FIVE! My heart sank. I knew it right away. It had to be us. It had to the 221st … DASPO (Department of the Army Special Photographic Office) was a possibility but generally they didn't have teams that large. And it was Pleiku.

I had spent nearly two months in Pleiku as OIC (Officer In Charge) of the detachment. I knew how the "slicks" – the choppers – coming into Pleiku often had to go "low level" to avoid friendly artillery fire. I hated that. I preferred flying at 5,000 feet, where the enemy could not reach you. I immediately placed myself back in Pleiku – on that chopper – auto-rotating down to low level, the doors opening, the door gunners swinging their .50-calibers out looking for trouble.

My body remembered the feeling – the feeling I had the very first time I flew low level. I thought it was kind of neat. An "E" ticket, like the best rides at Disneyland. You were whizzing over the canopy. You felt the speed. Whoopee. Ride 'em cowboy. Only later did I wise up. I realized they could hear you coming. They had time to aim. A lucky shot, a single bullet, might be enough to bring you down. After that realization, I hated flying low.

My heart jumped into my throat when, without warning, we swooped down on a river near Phu Bai. I even grew to dislike going low level to get our aerial shots of some godforsaken signal site near the DMZ. I remembered those particular times coming back from Kontum into Pleiku when we went low, again to avoid friendly fire. I pictured that. It was all too vivid.

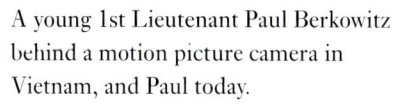

A young 1st Lieutenant Paul Berkowitz behind a motion picture camera in Vietnam, and Paul today.

I kept thinking, WHO? Who went down? Was it anyone I knew? FIVE OF OUR GUYS. It almost had to be someone I knew. BUT WHO? I had no way to find out. I couldn't sleep. I broke open the scotch.

In my mind then, the five photographers killed that day were ours. I had no way to confirm it – and I made no attempt either. I suppose I could have. But I didn't … just couldn't.

As the days and weeks went by, I put it out of my mind. Then, months later, I got a call from Bobo Swartz, my roommate in Long Binh. He had just returned home. It wasn't long before he told me I was right.

The one I knew best was Chris Childs. He had been with me in the Pleiku detachment. My eyes teared up. My voice cracked.

Childs. He had a wife and a baby at home. I had tried to stop him. I had trouble with him. He wanted to get "real" combat pictures. He was serious about an Army photo career. He kept going off on his own. He'd jump on the first 4th Div. MedEvac headed for a hot LZ. I had tried to keep him safe but I couldn't stop him. *Combat photography was our mission*. How could I keep him from it? Now he was dead.

And Doug Itri. Wasn't he that young, tall, friendly, skinny kid who wanted to be out in the field? The Colonel's pet? That's all I could remember. He was so friendly, we'd say hello and I knew he wanted out of Long Binh but the Colonel wouldn't let him go. But Doug had finally gotten his wish.

After talking to Bobo, I took a walk that night. I went around and around our block, thinking one thought. *I might have been on that chopper.* Those guys were part of the push into Cambodia. Bobo had said that nearly the whole company went, all the photo teams. If it wasn't for my emergency leave, I would have gone too.

I felt sure that Childs, Lowe and Paradis were from the Pleiku detachment. I was long gone, but to me that night, somehow they were still my guys. I kept thinking, thinking Yes – I could have been with them. But Bobo had said, "No officers were with them. You wouldn't have been with them. No way."

I couldn't shake it. Logic went out the window. To me, they were my team. I kept walking. Bobo had said that it was rumored that the guys had survived the crash and were "executed" on the ground. A horrible thought, that later we found out wasn't true. They all died in the crash, brought down by small arms fire. But that night, my imagination had no limits.

I pictured the whole thing, over and over, like a movie clip in an endless loop. I was helpless. I couldn't change a goddamn thing. I couldn't stop anything from happening. But the pictures kept coming. I kept walking with that one thought. *I was with them. I was with them.* Then I realized (as crazy as it sounds), that I always would be.

"Remembering Our Brothers" – Reflections by Members of the 221st Signal Company

"Ron Lowe and I were in the Mopic class from September to December 1969. Ron was one of five Army soldiers in the class. He was married and would get to Norfolk, Virginia as much as possible. When our school ended, I took him to Richmond to catch his ride home. We caught up with each other in the Oakland Army Depot. One night before we left, I called my new wife on the free phone system. Ron came with me; he took the phone to talk to Linda. She told him to watch out for her husband. Ron said he would and that we would look after each other. He died one month before his son was born. Five went over; four came back." – **Sp5 Nelson Thomas**

"I was the executive officer of the 221st Signal Co. (Combat Photo) when Doug Itri was killed. He was a good friend of mine. The last time I saw him was about two weeks before he was killed. I found him and Larry Young in the motor pool that evening and we had a couple of beers and just enjoyed the warm night air. Larry was one of the photographers killed in the helicopter with Doug. He was a terrific guy too. They all were." – **1st Lt. Robert "Bobo" Swartz**

"We both arrived at the 221st in early March 1970. Ray Paradis was assigned to the detachment in Pleiku and I was in Long Binh. He was a fairly quiet individual. He had an interest in hunting, fishing, and of course, photography. Living in New Hampshire he enjoyed driving through the countryside photographing small towns. He told me that most every small community had at least two beautiful churches, a town hall, and fire station. He was especially proud of the scenic beauty of the change of colors during the fall. He wasn't really sure that the Army would be a career for him but he was excited about being a combat photographer. He wanted to be a photojournalist or operate his own photographic studio when he returned to civilian life. My last conversation with him was in early May 1970. He was quite concerned that his next mission would be his last. I tried to reassure him that if he did his job and took no unnecessary chances he would be fine. I have always regretted that conversation with him." – **Sp5 Richard Jernigan**

"Larry Young was in the Americal Division and took an extension of his tour to be a photographer. I'm not sure where he was trained. Not by the Army, to the best of my knowledge. I think Larry joined us sometime in February or March of '70. He was not with us long prior to us losing him." – **Sp5 Ray Linn**

"Larry Young told me when he first came to the 221st he got a Bronze Star when he was with the Americal Division. He said that the trigger on his M-60 got stuck as they were retreating and it turned the fight around in their favor. I don't know if it was true or not; he said it jokingly. He also said that he extended his tour to get out of the Infantry ... he reenlisted as a photographer to get into the unit and out of the field with the Americal Division. I only got to talk to him a couple of times. I went to Bien Hoa Air Base for two weeks, on a shoot about Dog Training, shortly after he arrived. When I got back he & Ron Lowe had gone up to Pleiku." – **Sp5 Tom Kane** Photo by Evan Mower

"Doug Itri and I were friends in Vietnam. We often talked of 'meeting up' when he was discharged. He lived in Boston, I lived in New York City, and we both saw a good long friendship ahead. I remember receiving either a letter or phone call from John Lewis, I cannot recall which, he too was with the 221st. He had informed me of Doug's passing soon as it happened. I cried for a long time, and still do as we approach the anniversary day. I had visited the traveling 'Wall' when it passed through Atlanta, where I have been living. I sketched his name on a napkin. Sadly, it has been lost over the years. He was a hell of a guy." – **Sp4 Frank Cortellino**

"I knew them all – they were my guys. Everybody was just in shock when the word came back in, it hung over the place like the tomb of gloom. It was just awful. We did a memorial service for all of them. I did a eulogy. A lot of people showed up for that; we were in one of those units where people getting killed wasn't commonplace. It just stunned everybody. You always knew it could happen – but somehow it never did – then it finally did." – **Cpt. Bill Kelly**

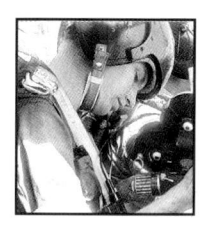

"We were on the way back to Pleiku (May 9, 1970) in a Chinook … the helicopter started circling. It was getting dark; (we) landed. I didn't know why until the crew chief said that everybody had to leave the ship. Some soldiers were to form a perimeter … everyone else was to go forward about a hundred yards to a downed helicopter … and find out if anyone had survived. Three of us got up there. It was obvious that the chopper had crashed. Most of the light, at that point, was coming from the phosphorous glow of the engine … like a beacon. We picked up some of the bodies and brought them back to the ship and then we went back for more. On the second trip back I noticed that there were a lot of silver film cans, and I noticed a patch on one of the soldiers who had perished and his patch matched the one I was wearing. And then I realized what had happened. It was completely deserted (at the crash site) … no enemy fire, no evidence of a battle. It was dusk. It was desolate. No sound of artillery … it was just very quiet. The chopper was totalled. The engine was destroyed. They probably perished due to the crash; no sign of blood or evidence of a firefight. It was very solemn."
– **1st Lt. Ken Hoffman, 221st Signal Co. MACV Team Leader**

A chaplain in Pleiku conducting services for the five combat photographers killed in the crash of GhostRiders 079. (*Photo by 1st Lt. Eric Wiegand, 221st Sig. Co.*)

Christopher J. Childs, III

Age 30

MOS: 84B20: Still Photographic Specialist

221st Signal Company (Pictorial)

Republic of Vietnam

Killed in *GhostRiders 079* shootdown

"His method was to go down to one of the 4th Div. headquarters and wait for something to happen in the field. He'd stay there all night if necessary and wait. When he heard that some "shit" was happening, he would go out on the first MedEvac chopper. Chris would get off as the wounded were getting on. His hope was that he could get into the action for some real combat shots." – Paul Berkowitz, 1st Lt., 221st Signal Company

Here are some of Chris's photographs, contributed by his son, Chris Childs IV, in memory of his father …

111-CCV-637

CC-267681

VIETNAM
CPT Larry Limars, (Fayetteville, N.C.) CO, Co "D", 502nd Inf, of the 173rd Airborne Bde, receives medical aid from SP5 William A. Hamsperger, (Cedar Rapids, Iowa) after a sniper ambush while on a search and secure mission north of the Ai Lao River, 50km northwest of Dong Song.

29 March 1970

Photo by SP4 Childs
221nd Sig Co.

AVRK-C-237-5/AGA 70
UNCLASSIFIED by USARA, 16 Jul 70

Ken Grissom

"I was in photo school at Fort Monmouth with Doug Itri and went on a couple of assignments with Chris Childs to cover the Montagnards near Pleiku. It was in the afternoon in Long Binh when we heard the news that they had been killed coming back from Cambodia, along with Paradis, Lowe and Young.

"All five had been killed ... never expected anything like that as we had only lost three photographers up until that time covering the war. We were in shock and one of Doug's close friends, don't remember his name, but he just fell on the ground crying. It was a very somber and depressing time, something I will never forget. After that it was so quiet. No one knew what to say ... what to do.

"At the request of Colonel Colville we assembled all the photos we could find and put them into books and I drew sketches of each of the guys on the cover, and they were sent to their families. Then I decided to combine sketches of all the guys into a memorial.

"I was in Doug's hometown of Boston in the mid-1980s on a construction project for about six months and started numerous times to call his family but just couldn't do it." –
Ken Grissom, 221st Signal Company

Douglas John Itri

Age 22

MOS: 84B20: Still Photographic Specialist

221st Signal Company (Pictorial)

Republic of Vietnam

Killed in *GhostRiders 079* shootdown

(*Photo by Evan Mower taken May 2, 1970*)

"I remember talking to Doug about photography maybe a couple of months before he was killed. He said to me, 'No matter what ever happens to me, my life is complete now that I'm a photographer.' I always remember that very vividly. It sticks with me. Once, while in Boston, I went to South Boston to the park he played in as a kid. His name is there on a plaque. That day, I just imagined him as a kid playing in that park. I so much miss Doug to this day. He was a great guy." – Spec. 5 Ray Linn, 221st Signal Company

The Leica camera assigned to Doug, with his last roll of film still in it, was retrieved at the crash site by Lt. Ken Hoffman. These are some of the last images Doug shot.

188   Cameras, Combat and Courage

Ronald Sidney Lowe

Age 21

MOS: 84C20: Motion Picture Specialist

221st Signal Company (Pictorial)

Republic of Vietnam

Killed in *GhostRiders 079* shootdown

The slate on these frames from the footage seems to indicate that it was shot by Ron Lowe, May 5, 1970, as part of the coverage of the Cambodian incursion. The description accompanying the footage reads: "UH-1H helicopters land at pickup zone in Cambodia. United States 101st Airborne Division and 4th Infantry Division soldiers board the helicopters. Helicopters lift off to advance into Cambodia."

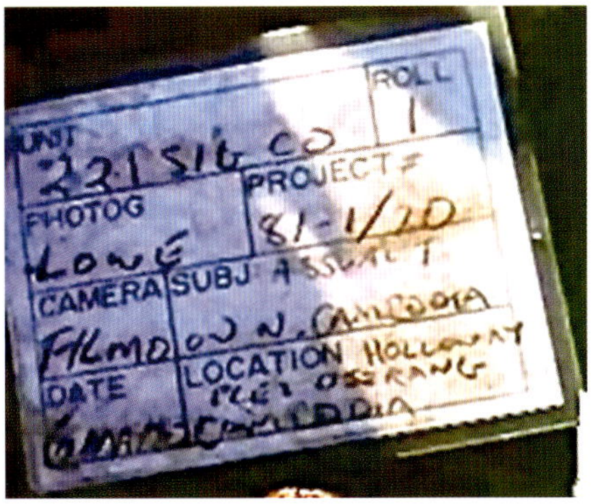
UNIT
221 SIG CO
ROLL
1
PROJECT #
81-1/20
PHOTOG
CAMERA
SUBJ
LOCATION
DATE

190   *Cameras, Combat and Courage*

Raymond Louis Paradis

Age 21

MOS: 84B20: Still Photographic Specialist

221st Signal Company (Pictorial)

Republic of Vietnam

Killed in *GhostRiders 079* shootdown

"Raymond was part of the Pleiku detachment along with Chris Childs and Ron Lowe. I found the mysterious picture at the top left of this page with the following caption: 'Memorial Day may be over, but memories of New Hampshire's war dead are kept alive at the War Memorial room at the Memorial Union Bldg. Recently, a visitor left this picture, of Raymond L. Paradis, a Nashua soldier who was killed in Vietnam in May 1970. Paradis was an Army photographer when the helicopter he was in was shot down as it returned to the Pleiku army base in Vietnam from a combat mission in Cambodia. The photograph, with a rubbing of Paradis's name taken from "The Wall" at the Vietnam War Memorial in Washington, D.C., included no note or clue as to who left it, or why.'" – Paul Berkowitz, 1st Lt., 221st Signal Company

Ghostriders 079   191

Some of Ray's photographs, from the National Archives …

Larry Clayton Young

Age 22

MOS: 84B20: Still Photographic Specialist

221st Signal Company (Pictorial)

Republic of Vietnam

Killed in *GhostRiders 079* shootdown

(*Photo by Evan Mower taken May 2, 1970*)

""I took this shot of Larry Young on May 2, 1970 exactly one week before he was killed. It was shot seconds after the shot of Doug Itri that's already in my collection. The two of them were sitting on the steps, chatting. It was fairly late in the afternoon." – Spec. 5 Evan Mower, 221st Signal Company

"That is Young. He told me when he first came to 221st that he got a Bronze star when he was with the Americal Div. He said that the trigger on his M-60 got stuck as they were retreating and he turned around. I don't know if it was true or not; he said it jokingly. He also said that he extended his tour to get out of Infantry. I remember seeing an Americal patch on his fatigues when he first came to the 221st. – Spec. 5 Tom Kane, 221st Signal Company

This picture of Larry Young was contributed by Tim Marks.

*"I believe it is one of the GhostRiders photographers.
It is the only pic I could get and
I wanted one to remember those guys."*

– Spec. 4 Tim Marks, 221st Signal Company

Sadly, to most of us, the word "Vietnam" first and foremost brings to mind a war. Just saying the word triggers images of combat, destruction, and suffering. But if you are Vietnamese, your first thoughts instead would most likely be of a country and a people with a great history and culture.

Fortunately, many of us who went to Vietnam as soldiers saw, if only briefly, the country hidden beneath the conflict. Most of us were young and in a strange land for the first time in our lives. Some of us found it fascinating and managed to see a country and its people hidden under the shadow of a brutal war.

Even a hardened combat veteran occasionally pointed a camera at some kids kicking around an old soccer ball in a jungle village or an aged farmer toiling in a rice paddy set against a beautiful exotic landscape of mountains covered in mist. Those of us who were fortunate enough to spend any time in a larger city, such as Saigon, brought home images of street vendors, historical landmarks of an ancient culture, artists and artisans, temples and more.

This brief gallery showcases some of that photography, mostly by those whose stories you've just read. It is a brief reminder of the times when we turned our cameras away from the killing and focused on the living. When we tried to capture and share our experiences of a land we sought to understand. And out of these photographs, that at the time were just snapshots to send home, comes a look at Vietnam – the country.

Vietnam ... was also a country.

Marvin Wolf

"A regular in a bustling little market that sprang up beneath the approach to a bridge over the Song Ba River leading to An Khe. His gnarled hands fascinated me."

"The Soc Trang Canal led from this provincial capital deeper into the Mekong Delta. Water taxis brought farmers and townies from around the low-lying province to conduct official and other business on the south bank."

"The Mango Lady was local color in a market in Bac Lieu, where I went in September 1966 to document the Constitutional Convention election."

"A lovely young Cambodian woman that I met in Da Lat while I was photographing the blossoms. She agreed to pose for a picture, then shyly disappeared."

"A winding path between rice paddies in Binh Dinh Province."

Tom Wong

"Everything in Vietnam was different from what I was used to, so it was easy to find something interesting to photograph. I had never been to a foreign country before, but it didn't take long to realize that people are the same, they just live their lives in different circumstances. It was the 'human interest' aspect of the Vietnamese people that interested me."

"I was wandering through a large indoor market in downtown Saigon when I saw this lady. There seemed to be a simple, elegant, peacefulness about her, and except for her clothing, she could have been a vendor at a farmers' market somewhere in America."

"This small market was not far outside the main gate of Tan Son Nhut. All the activity made it an interesting place to me."

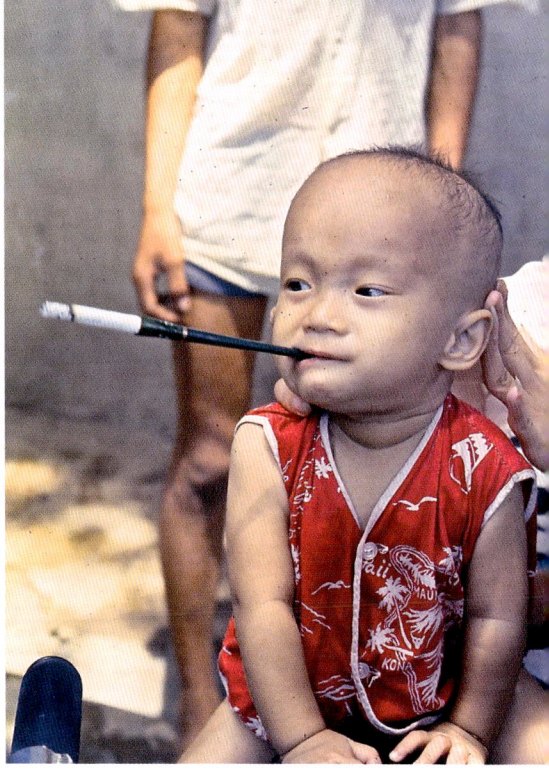

"If there was a baby around, the adults often preferred to stay out of the picture, and would try to get the baby to do 'cute' things like this."

"It was amazing to see how much the Vietnamese could carry, even young ladies like this one. All of this fit in the two baskets, that would then be hung from each end of a piece of bamboo, and carried on one shoulder."

"Kids will be kids – they want to get in the picture. These kids seemed to be as carefree, curious, and genuine as kids anywhere, in spite of the war."

Curtis D. Hicks (Rose)

"When I had the good fortune to catch this little 'Dancing Girl' on film I knew I had a treasure. Although life all around her was so much more difficult and ugly than anything I had ever dreamed of, she was still able to go dancing down the street in her own little world of 'childhood.'"

"This photo was taken from the balcony of a room a few of the guys from the Photo Platoon of the 69th Signal Battalion rented, just a few blocks from the main entrance to the Tan Son Nhut Air Force base."

"These three photos were taken at the 'Holy See' temple in Tây Ninh, It is the center of the main Cao Đàist church. I thought it was very interesting to see such wealth and splendor in the midst of people who were the poorest people I had even seen in my life."

James Saller

"I usually shot some photos like these when I was waiting around for someone or something. Or I was riding in the back of a truck in a convoy and saw what I thought might be an interesting picture. I might not always have had a loaded weapon with me, but I *always* had a loaded camera."

"These two photos were probably shot from a truck I was riding in. Roadside vendors were located at nearly every intersection outside of the villages, like these two girls selling vegetables. The lady carrying the baskets was probably bringing vegetables to some market."

"I think the boy was pouring rice into some kind of underground storage so it could be either hidden or preserved."

"I saw this Vietnamese man fishing in the river with a dip net. The bridge in the background was the result of sabotage by the NVA or Viet Cong."

Bill Perkins

Craig Ingraham

"Reading the letters that Bill sent home to his family was quite revealing. In his early letters, he referred to the Vietnamese people, as Marines learned to do, as 'gooks.' However, two months later, he referred to them as 'the Vietnamese.' It seems he was beginning to see them as human beings.

"His still photographs, like his motion-picture footage, revealed very little of the carnage of war. Mostly, they depicted the people of Vietnam and their way of life. And just like the Marines he photographed, he also made the Vietnamese people smile. Most compelling to me are his photographs of village life and a culture that has flourished for thousands of years. Though primitive by our standards, these resourceful, intelligent and wise people were able, in the twentieth century, to drive off the Japanese, French and the Americans.

"Though Bill was only in-country three months to the day before he died, his pictures reveal respect and even love for the Vietnamese people."

Editor's note: Craig Ingraham, a close friend of Bill Perkins, produced the documentary film, Above and Beyond: The Story of Corporal William T. Perkins, Jr. USMC. *Bill was a motion picture photographer with the marines, but also took the still photographs seen here. Today, Craig is the custodian of Bill's photographs and his letters to home. Corporal Perkins is the only combat photographer ever awarded the Medal of Honor.*

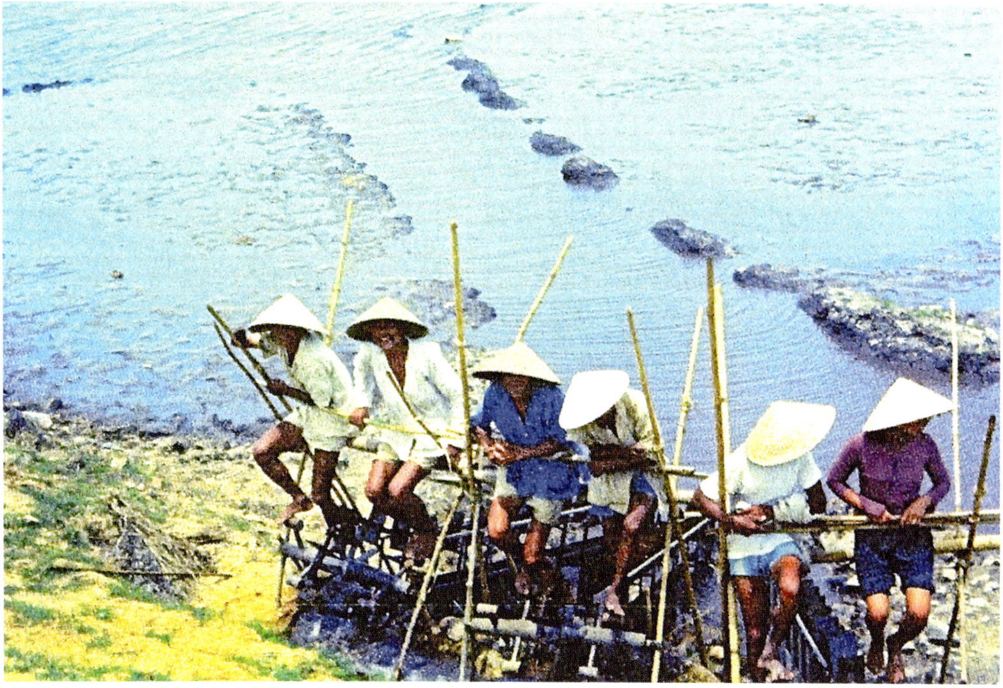

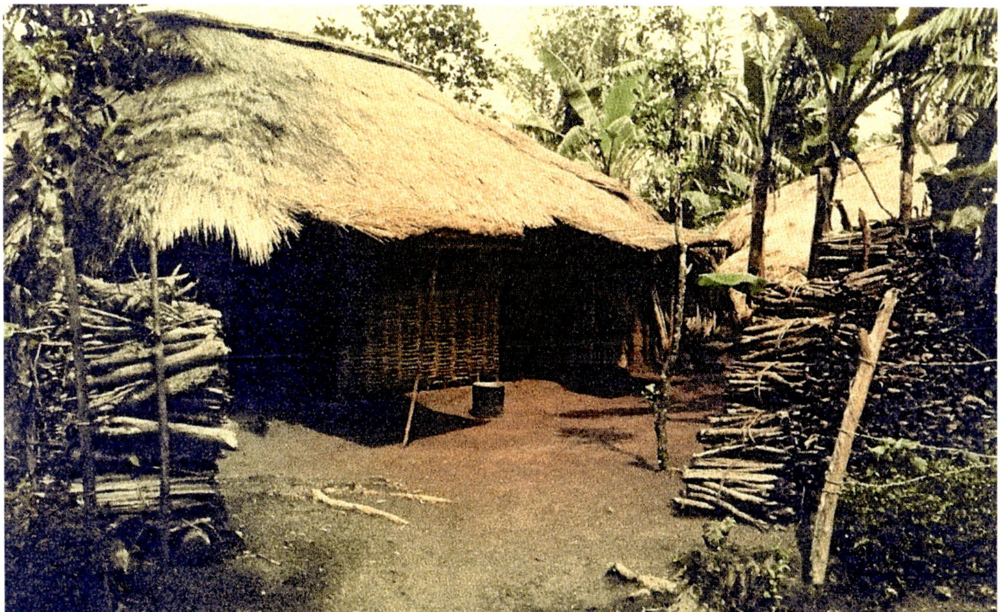

Roy McClellan

"A lot of the pictures I have of the people and country that weren't military in nature were taken in the city of Da Lat, up in the Central Highlands area of Vietnam This is one of the local streets.."

"A schoolteacher and one of her students. Those are rubber trees in the background."

"Two girls in traditional 'ao-dais' walking down a Da Lat street."

"A movie theater in Da Lat and a scene of the local marketplace. At nearly 5,000 feet elevation, Da Lat's temperate climate produces a wide array of vegetables, fruits, and flowers."

"Cam Ranh Bay frequently had some spectacular sunsets like this one I managed to catch one evening."

Bill Mondjack

"A beautiful, tranquil scene I took at the National Zoo in Saigon."

"I found this man resting in a Moslem temple in the Cholon district of Saigon."

"A mama-san and her children outside their village home in Gia Dinh Province, just outside of Saigon."

"I was mostly drawn to the people of Vietnam as the predominant subjects of my photography.

"The old man was tending these plants along a Saigon street.

"The lady with the umbrella, wearing a native dress known as an 'ao-dai' was shopping for plants or flowers during the Tet holiday, the Vietnamese Lunar New Year. Nguyen Hue Street was filled with vendors selling flowers and plants of every description.

"I photographed all these kids dressed in their uniforms and ready for classes outside their school in Cholon."

Afterword: Parting Shots

Dan Brookes

Author's note: This Afterword *originally appeared in* Shooting Vietnam, *the earlier companion volume to* Cameras, Combat and Courage. *I have chosen to repeat it here, not only because the reader may not have read* Shooting Vietnam, *but also because it is an important message and bears repeating …*

Vietnam was the most photographed war in history and will probably never relinquish that distinction.

Nothing escaped the camera in Vietnam. Between civilian and military photographers, millions of photographs and miles of film footage were taken.

The government and military wanted to document the war, bolster home support, and propagandize the noble effort it was making in the name of stopping communism in its tracks in southeast Asia. What better tool than the camera?

It failed, in both its public relations effort and the war itself. Instead, the camera helped kill the war.

"My greatest aim has been to advance the art of photography and to make it what I think I have, a great and truthful medium of history."
– Mathew Brady

"War is a monstrous piece of human stupidity. And I can't look at it any other way."
– Edward Steichen

Brady photo of a dead Confederate soldier after the Battle of Antietam.

Steichen photo of a dead Japanese soldier buried under the rocks and dirt after the Battle of Iwo Jima.

By the time the government and military figured out that the unbridled freedom they naively had given the media to support their propaganda effort had woefully backfired, it was too late.

The images of the war that became icons of the horror and brutality that was Vietnam had fueled an unstoppable anti-war movement. Instead of rallying the public to support the noble effort, it turned them against it.

Pictures like those taken by the war's civilian press photographers – Nick Ut's "Napalm Girl" and Eddie Adams' photograph of the execution of a Viet Cong prisoner in a Saigon street, for instance – combined with those of military photographer Ron Haeberle of the My Lai massacre of Vietnamese civilians by American troops, were never anticipated.

In Vietnam, truth finally triumphed over propaganda.

Many of the greatest war photographers sought to show the truth of war – its horror, suffering, desperation, and hopelessness. They captured everything that was terrible about war and placed it squarely in the public eye. It was impossible not to be affected by it. Civil War photographer Mathew Brady, seeking to show photography as "a great and truthful medium of history" did so by taking the dead of Antietam and figuratively laying them on the doorsteps of a shocked populace.

Even famed military photographer of the First and Second World Wars, Edward Steichen, hoped that photographs of wars somehow might prove to be a means to help end them. He called war "a monstrous piece of human stupidity" saying that he "can't look at it any other way." He felt tremendous guilt at the end of the First World War when he reflected back upon the aerial reconnaissance photography he had pioneered. He stated, "I could not deny to myself having played a role in the slaughter ... But the photographs we made provided information that, conveyed to our artillery, enabled them to destroy their targets and kill."

The military photographers who followed Steichen right to the present day, have never really been free to use their photographs for anything other than what the military allowed. All of the film shot by military photographers, including those in this book, was handed over to Signal Corps photo labs for processing and printing, and then matched up with the shooters' caption information. From the labs, all photos of a non-intelligence nature were sent up the chain of command to those who would decide whether they were useful for public release to the media or suitable for long-term storage in the National Archives; the rest were simply disposed of, destroyed.

The idea for this book began when after forty-plus years Bob Hillerby and I were reunited, totally by chance and, I have to say, by good fortune, through a website for veterans. Between us, we had managed to save hundreds of official military photos from possible destruction, in addition to still having our personal photographs, shot during our tours in Vietnam.

In our very first conversation after so many years, it became evident that we both had often thought about writing a book recounting our Vietnam experiences. I had always conceived my book as a look at the people and culture of Vietnam during the war, and not the war itself. Wanting Bob's story to be part of his family's legacy, they urged him for years to write about his time in Vietnam accompanied by his numerous photographs. We decided that our stories and photo collections complemented one another, and after many e-mails and telephone conversations, *Shooting Vietnam* was born.

I was a photo lab guy, more of what was commonly referred to as an REMF, a less than complimentary slang term for someone that was part of the rear echelons, and not out there in the field, in the thick of battle. In contrast, Bob spent almost all of his time in just the opposite role, primarily flying and photographing combat missions with the 1st Cavalry Division. More surprisingly, I never knew the details of Bob's time on the battlefield. Whenever we got together back in Saigon, he never talked about it and I didn't ask. We just ate, drank, roamed the streets of Saigon and did what we loved the most – took pictures.

While Bob wrote his story, he often would call me to talk about those battlefield experiences, sharing things I knew he would have rather kept buried, as he had struggled to do for so many years. Writing this, he said, was the hardest thing he had ever attempted.

As the book progressed, our research led us to others we had known and served with. We realized they had stories as well that covered a wide range of varying experiences. Soon we had a whole new mission for the book. Instead of just the stories and photographs of two buddies from Vietnam, we would have a book that represented, to the best of our ability, the war in Vietnam as seen through the eyes of its military photographers, told in their own words. Two voices had now become twelve.

I have already stated how difficult it was for many of those we connected with to dig so deeply into a past they would have rather not revisited. Fortunately, some did choose to go there, and for that we are greatly indebted to them. In these pages, they have shared their innermost thoughts and feelings about their time in Vietnam. Several told us that they were telling these stories for the very first time, talking about things that they hadn't even shared with loved ones.

The other driving force behind our choice to include them was to give them the recognition they so greatly deserved. Doing one's duty in the military is, for the most part, a thankless task. It's just expected. Yet, it was these photographers who, through their cameras, made their fellow GIs feel important, assuring them that they would do their best to bring their images to hometown newspapers, magazines, or the military's own publication, *Stars and Stripes*.

As Bob and I searched through the thousands of images stored in the National Archives, we were also able to unearth photographs that some of these photographers

Soldier in Vietnam reading the *Stars and Stripes*, the official armed forces newspaper published by and distributed only to the military.

had taken and allow them to see them for the very first time. The same was true of many of the photographs I had made extra copies of in the photo lab and brought home with me. When we shared them, a frequent response was, "Hey! I took that photo!"

Most of the military photographers in this book have written about their freedom to travel the war zone without very specific guidelines for what they were tasked to shoot. When they accompanied troops on combat operations, they developed closer relationships with fellow soldiers than their civilian counterparts could, and usually carried security clearances that gave them more access as well. Often, their photographs were deemed highly desirable by those outside the military, and there were generous offers from some reporters and photojournalists to buy finished prints or even just exposed rolls of film from military photographers. And of course sometimes the offers were motivated by their fear of covering dangerous, life-threatening battles and experiencing combat up close.

So what happened in Vietnam? How, after such strict censorship in past wars, did the Vietnam War become a photographic free-for-all?

At first, American forces in Vietnam were "advisers," not combat troops. We were the good-guy John Waynes in green berets sent there to show the Vietnamese how to fight the commies. No sinking of the Lusitania, no Pearl Harbor. In fact, as we know today, a lie fabricated by a desperate, conniving LBJ in the form of the Gulf of Tonkin Resolution of War was basically forced down the throats of a gullible populace to totally engulf us in the conflict.

A manufactured war required a massive public relations effort to sell it to the country and rally its support. So they called on the media with its own army of journalists, photographers, and cameramen to give their blessing to the cause. But to solicit a skeptical, post-Korea media meant granting it unprecedented access and freedom from any censorship at all.

Vietnam was also the first war to be no longer viewed in just newspapers and magazines; it would be seen by most through one of the 52 million TV sets that sat in nine out of ten homes at the start of the 1960s. The "living-room war" was born.

Vietnam was fought by a different generation, one that quickly developed a cynicism and doubt about the entire war. This attitude occasionally crept into the military's own media, like the *Stars and Stripes* newspaper publication. Written by an amalgam of civilian and military personnel, it is still distributed only among the military. It operates through the Department of Defense and is even protected by the First Amendment.

During the Vietnam War it often rankled senior officers with its candid, no-bullshit approach to reporting news of the war. One particular example is an article about an infantry company during a battle at Hiep Duc, written and photographed by Specialist 4th Class Bob Hodierne that appeared in the August 31, 1969 issue.

Hodierne told the story of an intense battle that left an infantry company tired, frightened, and dispirited. It caused an uproar throughout the top Army command in Vietnam, especially since at the time over 100,000 copies a day of the *Stars and Stripes* were distributed to troops in Vietnam.

Eight days later, the Associated Press (AP) distributed an article to stateside newspapers that said, "The US High Command in South Vietnam is so incensed with news reports appearing in the Pacific *Stars and Stripes*, the US armed forces newspaper in Asia, that it has started calling it the 'Hanoi Herald.'" Colonel James Campbell, chief spokesman for the US Army command in Vietnam said, "It is the opinion of USARV that such stories do not border on treason – they are treason."

Colonel Campbell also commented, "Nobody in USARV is trying to muzzle the press ... Nobody expects *Stars and Stripes* to be a smile sheet and report only tapioca news. But the Army does expect – and is not getting – a fair shake from the *Stars and Stripes*."

Specialist 4th Class Hodierne's frank reporting about the battle, as well as his photographs that accompanied it, were unsettling. The brass considered his article demoralizing. A war that was already being harshly criticized by the civilian media was bad enough; it wasn't going to tolerate the same from its own publication.

In addition to the hundreds of military photographers in Vietnam, cameras were carried by the majority of other GIs as well. Many of their photographs reflected the horror of what they experienced. In a post to the *Nieman Reports* website in 2000, Steve Northup, a United Press International (UPI) photographer in Vietnam during 1965 and 1966, talked about soldiers he met:

"At almost every small outpost I went to, some GI would come over and want to show me his snapshots. And nine times out of 10, they were truly disturbing. Body parts,